A SYSTEMIC HARPOON INTO FAMILY GAMES

Preventive Interventions in Therapy

A SYSTEMIC HARPOON INTO FAMILY GAMES

Preventive Interventions in Therapy

by

GIULIANA PRATA, M.D.

BRUNNER/MAZEL, *Publishers* · New York

Library of Congress Cataloging-in-Publication Data
Prata, Giuliana.
    A systemic harpoon into family games : preventive interventions in
therapy / by Giuliana Prata.
        p.   cm.
    Includes bibliographical references.
    Includes index.
    ISBN 0-87630-591-5
    1. Family psychotherapy.   2. Interpersonal relations.   3. Family
psychotherapy—Case studies.   I. Title.
    [DNLM: 1. Counseling—methods.   2. Family Therapy—
methods.
3. Interpersonal Relations.   WM 430.5.F2 P912s]
RC4880.5.P725   1990
616.89'156—dc20
DNLM/DLC
for Library of Congress   90-2157
                                                                          CIP

Published by
BRUNNER/MAZEL, INC.
19 Union Square West
New York, NY 10003

Manufactured in the United States of America

10   9   8   7   6   5   4   3   2   1

To My Parents

Contents

Preface

The idea of writing this book occurred to me in Finland, in August 1986, during a workshop organized by the Family Therapists' Association and the Association for Mental Health.

Obviously, there is a great difference between thinking about writing a book and actually writing it. I am glad I made this effort, because it obliged me to synthesize my reflections and research work in family therapy, testing those ideas with theoretical fundamentals and clinical results.

One may ask why I included so many transcriptions of family sessions. This book was written for professionals who every day, within either the public or the private sector, meet families, couples, or individual patients. My main concern was to supply less experienced colleagues with a working tool which could help them on a clinical level. Moreover, the transcriptions of certain sessions can be as exciting as a theatrical script. Actually, after seeing one of our sessions in Milan, Arthur Penn exclaimed: "Those sessions are more dramatic than any theatre performance!"

I gave less importance to the theoretical aspect of the therapeutic situation than to its clinical aspect, because there are many excellent theoretical books and articles which explain the *whys and the wherefores* of given behaviors and suggest *what to do* to change them. Yet, as a therapist, I often feel embarrassed concerning the *how* to face a situation, make an investigation, or carry out an intervention. For instance, *how to proceed* in order to "put the blame on the absent," "make hypotheses and test them," "use neutrality and circular questioning as instruments to get information" and so on? The question may sound elementary, but it is not, and the therapist may have problems in *putting it into practice*.

Usually, couples seem less intimidating than families and, similarly, individual patients seem less intimidating than couples. Nevertheless, individual patients sometimes manage to involve the therapist in such a way that they are able to neutralize his or her therapeutic resources more successfully than a family. The reason is that, when dealing with a family, the therapist is more afraid of the possibility that he/she might be overwhelmed by the number of people involved than when treating a single patient and is thus more watchful. Yet one ought to consider each and every case as difficult and never relax one's vigilance until the therapy has come to an end. In fact, all our patients are involved in "games" from which we should help them to extricate themselves without getting enmeshed ourselves. And that is not an easy task.

I must say that it was not difficult for me to adopt in my practice and in my writings a pragmatic attitude. This was probably due to the fact that before becoming a family therapist I was trained as a medical doctor. Clinical examples will help me explain the conviction I have reached. Actually, over the past few years, my main working hypothesis has been:

> *Mental illness does not exist. Symptoms appear when a family develops an excessive passion for playing "games" and one of its members is losing heavily, not because the strongest wins but because someone is rigging the stakes and cheating.*

When a man and a woman marry, amidst the furniture they bring into their new house, there is the invisible but always present "green table." They both bring in some gambling chips and immediately start playing their "games," not only the "games" they have learned from their respective families but also their very own new "games." From time to time they will return to their family homes, separately or together, to sit at their family's "green table" to play the original family game or to relaunch it in a new form. Returning to their new home, they can double the minimum stake and enjoy the risks involved in their game.

Most of these people go on forever amusing themselves and their children. Within other families, someone makes "the move" which spoils the "game" or the rules change at a certain point. Husband and wife become enmeshed, persist, and refuse to leave the "green table." No one wants to be excluded. The children, contrary to the linear way of thinking, are never passive, innocent members of the family. There are neither victims nor active victimizers. There are only players! The more one loses, the more he will become stubborn, fierce, and systemically stupid.

I believe in free will; therefore, I believe that when a player doesn't leave the field it's because he doesn't want to, not because he is a "poverino." When a player has his back to the wall, is being set up to lose, and everyone has turned against him, someone begins to cheat and win heavily, which makes the game more intense. Thus, the game turns into an escalation and the stakes become higher and higher. Finally, the game becomes cruel, with no one willing to leave the "green table," neither the winner nor the loser.

Then the winner starts boasting. The challenge becomes so intense for the loser that leaving at that moment is simply too painful and difficult. How can one leave the field when feeling so outrageously mortified! The loser hopes for a chance rescue and tries to win the children to his/her side. But why would the children-players *truly* side with a loser? Feeling totally isolated, depleted, and down, the loser will ally himself with symptoms in an attempt to acquire some power. In the majority of cases, the parents are the winner and the loser, while the children, aware of the power they wield over the split couple, start playing for themselves against their parents. There will be other winners and other losers.

This conception of family systems is the epistemological paradigm which has ruled my work over the last years. Nevertheless the content of this book is not meant to be a scientific demonstration of its validity.

Khun (1962), Lakatos (1976), and other famous epistemologists have already underscored the fact that science is always developing on foundations which are not yet scientific. However without such foundations, no research program would ever be feasible. Without them, we would actually lack the substantial element on which the investigation has to be focused—that is, the choice of *what to look for.*

When I say: "The game has taken possession of the family," I want to make clear that the game is not some strange bird of prey flying destructively at the family. What hurled itself into the family was a misfortune, not a sinister "dirty game."

That paradigm has become, to me and to my team, the clue to deciphering family systems. Thanks to that paradigm, we have been able to bring to the fore some "regularities" within the patterns of disturbed families which were helpful in guiding our therapeutic interventions. In my opinion, what is important to assess and take into account is the pragmatic effectiveness of our actions. It is this effectiveness, which, after all, is valued by the families themselves now and in the future. Besides, our follow-ups support me in the apparently hard way in which I act.

Supposedly, I am a moral person trying to avoid moralism. In order not to moralize, I should perhaps refer only to entertaining, painful, or difficult games. But when I say "dirty games," it's because the consequences have struck a linear cord in my soul. I try to use the term only during team discussions which are linear at the beginning and, as they go on, become more circular until they reach a systemic conclusion. I also term the game as "dirty" to the family when my aim is to give that family game a systemic blow.

My colleagues regard me as drastic and hard. This doesn't surprise me at all. I am! However, what they don't take into account is my empathy for the family. I make strong statements only to break the game, not to offend the participants. The title of this book should be: "I must be cruel, only to be kind" (Hamlet: III, 4), but the meaning would be obscure except to my patients, my cotherapists, and my students who have knowledge of the experience.

Acknowledgments

I want to thank my Finnish friends in the family therapy field, as well as:

- Dr. Mara Selvini Palazzoli for sharing with me 14 years of research work;
- Dr. Odette Masson for her friendly support;
- Drs. Paola di Blasio, Jean Marc Fischer, and Elida Romano;
- Esme Gotz and Esther Gelcer, who first suggested to me to write a book;
- Mr. Arnold Pomerans for his help;
- Miss Soghra M. Sadeghi for doing the editing and the Index;
- Mrs. Maria Antonietta Milcovich, Mrs. Giuliana Paramithiotti, and Mrs. Enrica Dal Pont Solbiati for their generous assistance in putting the manuscript in order;
- Mr. Norman F. Stevens for his help;
- Drs. Cinzia Raffin and Susana Frondizi Bullrich, my research associates;
- Drs. Luisa Bigoni Prata and Maria Vignato Chinaglia, my cotherapists and victims, for their support and helpful criticism.

No wind serves him who addresses
his voyage to no certain port.

—Seneca

1

Introduction to a Systemic Style of Counseling

Starting in 1972, I became a member of the research group called the *Centro per lo Studio della Famiglia di Milan.* The other members of this team were Drs. Selvini Palazzoli, Boscolo, and Cecchin. We were all psychiatrists and psychoanalysts with very active practices. Dr. Selvini and I had some experience in family therapy. For each one of us, psychoanalysis, as it was being used in family therapy, had become obsolete and ineffective. We began the search for a new idea which could deal with the family as a living system and produce basic, structural, therapeutic changes.

This "new instrument," which could cure systems, was not easy to develop since we were looking for a theory every bit as pure and rigorous as psychoanalysis. The trial test with psychoanalysis having proved to be an error, we decided to continue our experiment with the "General System Theory" (Bertalanffy, 1968) and rule out other theories as a basis for family therapy. To our mentors, Searles and Wynne, we added Bateson, Jackson, Haley, and Weakland (1956) and the other researchers of the Palo Alto Group, as well as Crozier and Friedberg (1977), Le Moigne (1977), Morin (1973, 1977, 1980, 1982, 1986), and others too many to name here. The reader will find them in the References.

Quite soon, a new understanding of relationships, double binds

1

(Sluzki & Veron, 1971; Bateson et al., 1956), and paradoxes within the family system encouraged us to continue in this direction. Since our choice was proving to be useful and effective, this became an exhilarating period of our experience as therapists and researchers, a time of creation and invention. The pleasure we felt during this first pioneering phase was reflected in our book *Paradox and Counterparadox* (Selvini Palazzoli, Boscolo, Cecchin, & Prata, 1978a) and in the articles of that same period. The most important one, "Hypothesizing—Circularity—Neutrality: Three Guidelines for the Conductor of the Session" (Selvini Palazzoli et al., 1980b), was also the last article we wrote together as a four-member team. By the time *Family Process* published it, Drs. Boscolo and Cecchin had separated from Selvini and myself and left the field of research to devote themselves entirely to training. Thanks to their teaching activity, we now have in Italy a new generation of well-trained family therapists.

The "New Method" (Selvini Palazzoli & Prata, 1982a) was introduced in 1979 and focally condensed our previous results. The work became even more interesting and rich with positive responses. In fact, it proved more effective than paradoxical therapy and we shifted definitely to this prescriptive one. Our explanation for its greater effectiveness was that a family can easily disconnect itself and cut off a verbal message, but once engaged in an action it cannot disconnect itself. Its members act or refuse to act. In either case, the therapist will receive important information because an action is always a more powerful input than a word.

We decided to leave the children at home after the second session and give the parents, in each session, something specific to do with the children: the secret, the evening disappearances, the weekends, and the long disappearance. We also gave the parents something specific to do for us. They had to write feedback notes and bring them to the session.

Not only the content but also the form of the *notes* became information for us. They could be concise or long, accurate, winded, endless, chaotic, scribbled, or even empty, but they always contained valuable information. Slowly the parents' *notes* became shorter and more interesting than they were at the beginning. We were probably also communicating more clearly what we wanted.

Another reason for shifting from a paradoxical therapy to a prescriptive one was "the extent of the effort required from the team, when faced with the difficulty of discovering in each family, especially in the family with schizophrenic organization, the specific ongoing game." There was also the fact that "giving the schizophrenic families a fixed, invariable prescription structures a repeatable therapeutical context. This repeatable context provides the optimal condition to learn about schizophrenia" (Selvini Palazzoli & Prata, 1982a). I don't want to quote more from the "New Method," but want only to reiterate that 1979 started the second phase of my experience as a researcher, which was to continue for seven fruitful years.

In October 1982, Dr. Selvini Palazzoli and I founded the *Nuovo Centro per lo Studio della Famiglia*. This center was dedicated to therapy and research on the premise that theory provides therapy with the necessary operational tools, and therapy in turn allows the therapist to submit theories to continuous testing (Viaro & Leonardi, 1986). Those theories and tools which might prove useless or incorrect can be discarded and replaced by others which seem more useful and appropriate. This is the most fascinating, though the most irritating, aspect of our research, both for us and for our colleagues, who watch us switch theory and techniques frequently. But this is precisely what characterizes true, live, ongoing research, research that evolves continually, requiring at every step a huge effort of the imagination and much theorizing. You grope your way forward painstakingly, and although every now and then you make a leap forward, you must be prepared at all times to face embarrassing and discouraging hitches and setbacks.

I left the New Center in June 1985, and founded my *Centro di Terapia Familiare Sistemica e di Ricerca* in September 1985. It is a private center, independent from any state or private financial support. Families request family therapy directly. The standard procedure is the following: Someone phones asking for an appointment and the secretary arranges for a second call to be made at a fixed time. The applicant then talks directly to one of the therapists. I wrote an article, together with my cotherapists Di Blasio and Fischer, entitled "The Telephone Chart: A Cornerstone of the First Interview with the Family," which was presented in Zurich, in

September 1985. This paper was then published by the *Journal of Strategic and Systemic Therapies* (Di Blasio, Fischer, & Prata, 1986) and explains the importance of the first contact with a family. Basically, it provides one with an outline on which to postulate the "gaming" hypothesis of the family.

When filling out these charts, I am active; that is, I ask the questions, and from this very first contact onward, take charge of the relationship with the family and their situation regarding therapy. I believe if this is not done the therapist can only fail to obtain the relational information necessary to draw up hypotheses about the dysfunctional patterns in the family. Bateson says that information is obtained through differences (1972b) and comparisons (1972a): if the therapist lets the caller ramble on freely, he will receive only this particular person's linear view of the situation. The chart, too, will turn out to be linear and devoid of useful information. The same thing will occur if the therapist collects only essential data and fills out a bureaucratic chart.

Actually, the information we really need concerns the relationships within the family system and the changes that occurred in these relationships during the past years or immediately prior to the appearance of the symptoms. The relationships that set in *after* the appearance of the symptoms are less important, since they are repetitive and simply follow the rules of whatever ongoing "game" is being played, for example, the "anorexic game," the "psychotic game," the "autistic game," and so on. In other words, we try to discover what particular changes in the family relationships brought on the Identified Patient's (I.P.) rebellion.

Often, our inquiry in cases of psychosis yields the forgotten or hidden information that something happened at the very onset of the problem, which we term "unusual behavior." For instance, it could have been a written message of complaint and revolt addressed to one of the parents, or a clearly defiant attitude, even in a very young child. All those initiatives may provide suitable channels for rebellion and obtain the desired changes. When the system is not too tightly entrenched in a repetitive "game," things can go back to normal in this way without any outside help. However, should the protest fail to bring about the hoped-for result, or actually produce exactly the opposite one, this sets off an escalation, and the ongoing "game" will become ever more dogged and relentless. Whereupon, there will be more dramatic symptoms leading to a request for therapy.

We also carefully look into events preceding or coinciding with the appearance of symptoms, such as the death of a "prestigious" grandmother who favored the identified patient. This may have left him/her without an ally and lowered his/her value on the "family market." The marriage of a sibling can also provide a clue to the underground network of favoritism and/or shift in the distribution of economic advantages, which, up to the time, had been sufficiently balanced out. Events that occurred prior to the manifested symptoms should be investigated very carefully during the session and placed in their proper historical and evolutionary perspective regarding the family system. Changes in family relationships, where the birthright of one sibling was given to another, or the shift/breaking up of an alliance, must be explored. Even a minute coincidence may have played an important part in tilting the "homeostasis" of the family.

The telephone chart (Di Blasio, Fischer, & Prata, 1986) allows the possibility of discussing which members of the extended family play important roles. Then we can summon these members to the first session. Relatives cohabiting with the nuclear family must come. We summon a member of the extended family only when we consider it helpful to better examine the problem. Usually such members are invited only to the first session and are then bid goodbye, in a friendly but conclusive manner.

Once the data have been collected, we sketch out a hypothesis and draw up the program for the session. Next, we must decide what questions are to be asked, in what order, and to whom they are to be directed. For instance, in case the father was the person who supplied the entries for the chart but has shown himself to be indirect and used this as a tactic for never coming to the point, we address certain questions to the mother, to a member of the extended family, or even to one of the offspring. When a session is carefully prepared, it becomes highly informative both for ourselves and the family.

Be careful not to invite members of both extended families together! This is a tactical error. It is an established fact that, in all cases relating to disturbed families, the relationships between the two families of origin or between the latter and the nuclear family members tend to be conflicted. If both extended families are required to attend the same session, they will spend most of their time keeping tabs on each other. The members of the nuclear family will fail to cooperate with the therapist and will be reticent, disqualifying, or supercilious towards him/her, not out of any personal animosity towards the therapist, but merely to reassure the members of the extended family who are present, showing that they assign no particular worth to the therapist. They may also use this attitude to avoid supplying the members of the extended family with useful playing cards. Obviously, the therapist may be disqualified and fail to obtain information even if one invites only the members of *one* extended family, but this is unfailingly the case when both families of origin are summoned together.

PSYCHOANALYSIS AS A THERAPEUTIC INSTRUMENT DESIGNED FOR THE ANALYST-PATIENT DYAD

Psychoanalysis treats individuals on the basis of a dyadic rapport and well-defined rules, using the analysis of transference and countertransference as its principal instrument. However, a therapist who wishes to use psychoanalysis to treat a family of, say, six members, will have to analyze six transferences plus six countertransferences and their evolution (Jackson & Haley, 1963). Needless to say, this will be not only hopelessly laborious, but also meaningless. Besides, digging into the deepest depth of each "soul" to seek out precocious traumatisms and "introjected figures" will inevitably lead the therapist to overlook the patient's present relationships with his family, the ongoing "game" within the family, and the constrictive rules of that "game."

After innumerable sessions, the therapist will certainly reach a better understanding of the "soul" of each of his clients, but will find himself ensnared with conversations and understandings which, in most cases, fail to induce any change whatsoever in the family functioning. "Family therapy is not psychoanalysis. The transference neurosis of psychoanalysis does not develop; in fact, its development is discouraged" (Mildefort, 1982, p. 2).

Being a psychoanalyst, I am fully aware that the I. P. has incorporated a world of childhood experiences into which, if we were in the dyadic setting peculiar to individual analysis, I would have to delve very deeply indeed, but which I cannot and must not deal with when the situation involves family therapy.

The question remains: What shall we do with all these incorporated experiences while working with the family? The systemic model is based on the cybernetic principle of stochastics—of, or pertaining to, a process involving a randomly determined sequence of observations, each of which is considered a sample of one element from a probability distribution. This means that when a baby is born, it comes into a family that has already set a number of rules governing the way its members live together. At this point, the baby appears, who is anything but a passive recipient of this status quo. It starts effecting a number of trials in order to explore the diverse ways in which it can place itself within the framework of its family and deal with those rules. It tries to understand what "moves" it can afford to make and which ones are to be avoided. In the stochastic process, this is known as the learning context (Bateson, 1972b). A child makes a choice after each "trial": it commits to memory and repeats the "moves" that have produced suitable results and eliminates the unsuitable ones.

If the rules of the family "game" are clear and not too rigid, the family will function well, incorporating the child in a satisfactory manner. Conversely, if the rules are rigid and confusing, the family's functioning will be severely hampered and tied to dysfunctional rules that render it even more problematic. Every individual during infancy constructs and interiorizes premises which then convert into self-fulfilling prophesies. For example, if a girl is convinced she is unattractive and goes to a dance, she will signal to everyone present, through her behavior, that she is ugly, and will sit out the entire evening as a wallflower. If a boy has learned within the "learning context" of his family that the "depression ploy" brings about the best results, he will resort to this "depression" maneuver whenever faced with difficulties and will expect everyone to pay attention.

Obviously, we are referring to relational problems, not to material difficulties. One may well ask: "Why are we able to achieve in a few sessions based on systemic therapy the results which formerly, in case we were lucky, would have required three hundred sessions?" In my opinion, when one is able to figure out the "game" and give a prescription which provides a patient with an experience which, within his or her framework of relations, would be unthinkable, a dramatic change is bound to occur. For example, when a child is looked upon as slightly retarded and everyone believes that it is necessary to constantly protect him, at home and in school, his general state will steadily deteriorate. The child will fall behind at school, becoming generally less and less capable of coping with life. The final results will probably be an enormous amount of money spent on remedial schooling.

If possible, we avoid seeing this type of child. He has already been mortified and made to feel "different" by a series of specialists and stacks of mental aptitude tests. Therefore, we try working solely with the parents, persuading them to change the child's environment by taking him out of the overly protective school and sending him to some other school. We strongly recommend that they do not hurry along and explain "the case" to the teaching staff. If the move works, the child, thanks to the parents, will enjoy the experience of a school where no one protects him and where he is treated just like the others (Selvini Palazzoli, 1985b).

In this new situation, many of the infantile experiences will be contradicted by a total set of new and different ones. The child can acquire a new value which was not part of his past or environment. Once acquired, the experience becomes a part of the entire family's experiential stock-in-trade. By virtue of its successful outcome, this new "trial" is committed to memory and preserved, correcting previous negative experiences. The former ones will appear as negative "trials" with a negative outcome or as "errors" to be discarded.

THE SYMPTOM AS A "MOVE" IN THE FAMILY "GAME"

We know that the symptom is not a gratuitous expression on the part of the I.P., disjointed from the context in which it appears. It is a signal that something is out of order, but it is a coded message. It hints at problems which, at the same time, it carefully helps to keep under cover. In any case, it is obvious that the symptom means something and has a purpose.

In individual analysis, it was quite common, once the symptom disappeared, to see others crop up to take its place, either in the I.P. or in another member of the family. Why does this usually fail to happen in the case of systemic individual and family therapy? Because we regard the symptom as a "move" and use it as the clue that can lead us to the discovery of the family's main "game" (Berne, 1974). When we succeed in changing this "game," neither the I.P. nor any other member of the family needs to resort to other symptoms signaling a distress which has vanished with the disappearance of the "pathogenic game" itself.

At times, the family's behavior and its analogic messages lead us to suspect that the "game" hasn't really changed, but the family has merely "frozen" it. At this point, if the family shows itself pleased with the results that have been forthcoming, I don't insist, but simply assign an appointment in six months' time "to see how things are going." If the symptom's disappearance is nothing but what we term "the escape-into-recovery" gambit, designed to cover up conflicts not yet resolved, such camouflage will not stand the test of time.

If, after six months, this "freezing of the game" still goes on and the parents agree factually that the problem has been overcome, it is obvious that they do not wish to continue therapy. If their behavior then bears out the hypothesis that the "game" has really not been changed and may not even have been touched on, I cannot force them to keep on with therapy. In such cases I simply say: "Our team has taken due notice of what you've told us. We would like to see you again in six months' time, just to see how things are going." It is very difficult to keep a problem "frozen" for a whole year. Sooner or later, something will seep through to the surface. Someone will make a more symmetrical and/or disturbing move, which will relaunch the escalation and make an old or new symptom appear.

If the family counters by shifting the responsibility of continuing or interrupting therapy onto my shoulders, obviously a symmetrical move, it would be useless to suggest regular meetings. They would only be designed to disqualify me and would shortly be followed by a dropout. I would not have solved the family's problem and would be responsible for the dropout. Therefore, I stick firmly to what they report and to my offer of a meeting in six months' time.

When the therapy is achieving good results and significant changes are occurring, it is best for the therapist to downplay these results during the first phase of therapy. Enthusiastic comments about the I.P.'s improvement, especially in the I.P.'s presence, may trigger the I.P.'s symmetry and a relapse. In fact, a satisfied attitude is inadvisable even when only the parents are present, seeing that they never really tell the therapist *everything!* Downplay the improvements! The family may be led to tell one something more, to prove that they are right and that the changes have really taken place. Sometimes, they reveal very important things, such as the fact that the I.P. not only is eating but is menstruating again after years of amenorrhea. If I am applying the prescriptive method and the parents are complying diligently, I chalk up the good results to them and attribute the failures to the I.P.'s resistance, mainly alleging that he/she does not want to give up his/her own "pathological power."

If the parents have been quarrelling, I try to discover what the causes and the surrounding circumstances are, whether this took place in the I.P.'s presence or not, and if it might have been the I.P. who caused the disagreement. Have the parents been taken for a ride? Did the I.P. manage to split them up, pitting one against the other to overtrump them separately, according to the old tactic of "divide et impera" ("divide and rule")? I tell them to pay close attention and notice if, whenever they squabble, the I.P. gets involved, directly or indirectly. A positive answer proves that the I.P. hasn't given up and they aren't out of the tunnel. In case they stop at that stage, they run the risk of backsliding.

If the parents demonstrate their gratitude for all my help, I feel it is still best to thank them, but to attribute most of the credit back to them, saying they could have decided not to carry out the prescriptions and, in that case, there would have been no change. This answer is not only quite truthful but tactically useful, because parents are willing to cooperate with someone more "qualified" than they are (by virtue of proper professional training). However, if one claims all the credit, there is the risk of arousing their symmetry.

To avoid stimulating the family's resistance, I don't suggest siding openly with change. Paradoxically, I will propose homeostasis, at least during the first session, which I tell the family is exploratory and meant to decide whether or not family therapy is suitable. Obviously, these sessions are already "therapeutic" and must be conducted in a very dynamic way, providing the family and the therapist with as much information as possible. This consequently allows me, with luck, to discover the family's "game" and rules.

If I decide to undertake family therapy according to the New Method (Selvini Palazzoli & Prata, 1982a), I make a therapeutic intervention on each of the offspring at the end of the second session, not on the I.P. alone. This means that, before excluding the "offspring" subsystem, I try to get at the "game" the children are playing amongst themselves and with the parents. Such an intervention may at times be efficient, especially when it is followed by the exclusion of the offspring during the next session. I come back into the room at the end of the second session to say that family therapy has been considered suitable in their case and tell the offspring, one by one, in order of age, that they are to stay home and that only their parents will be coming to the following session.

When family therapy is not suitable, as for example in the case of a prestigious referring sibling (Selvini Palazzoli, 1985a), I nonetheless hold two sessions. These yield more information than just one, and the second allows me to check whether the hypotheses drawn up and tested during the first session are correct or not. In fact, there is always the possibility for the therapist to go off tangentially and influence the family, inducing its members to respond in one way rather than another. After a month's interval, however, both the therapist and the family will have had time to reflect and reach different conclusions. Then, in this second session, the family has the opportunity to contradict the therapist's hypotheses and one can draw up and make adjustments to the new feedbacks (Raffin, 1988).

One has to be adroit even in the initial telephone conversation in order not to let the "symptoms" be a controlling factor. A short while ago, a call came from an I.P. who has had special problems with food for 24 years. She is an "ex-anorexic," age 38. Presently she is again refusing the food her mother prepares, as well as any other "normal" food. This bout has been going on for the past 12 months. But, at the same time, she keeps stuffing herself with things found in the garbage on the street.

She was screaming and weeping while I was filling out the telephone chart. I asked her to phone back five days later to arrange an appointment. The next day, however, she phoned me, demanding an urgent appointment immediately! I repeated my request for a call in five days' time, given that I was not able to tell her at that moment when I could arrange a family meeting. She started crying profusely, moaning that she simply couldn't wait any longer. I responded, "Well, after all, it's only a matter of eating out of the garbage pail for a few more days." Immediately, this stopped her whining and she replied, "No, doctor, you see, ever since I spoke to you yesterday I've stopped eating out of the garbage pail." "Anyway, I'm sorry but I can't tell you anything definite until Monday," I replied, and hung up.

Monday at the agreed time, I gave her the information and there were no more scenes. It may or may not have been true that she'd stopped eating out of the garbage pail. The point is, she found out, in contrast with other therapists and her family, who took her behavior most seriously and were appalled by the garbage-pail menu, that the ploy didn't impress me. Actually, on the completion of the "Telephone Chart," I had already formulated the hypothesis that the I.P., who was the daughter of a well-known doctor, with one brother an endocrinologist, the other a dentist, and a brother-in-law a psychologist, had been mortifying, humiliating, and "showing up" not only her "perfect" mother but all the prestigious therapists in the family. Besides, no doctor manages to be entirely free of fears regarding microbes and germs. With this ploy (and she had others!), she managed to get everyone frantically worried and thoroughly ashamed. She was carrying out real vengeance on the entire lot of them at one fell swoop—father, mother, brothers, sister, and brother-in-law.

Any "anorexic" family which has in its history a member (a daughter, a son, perhaps a mother) on a hunger strike and requests therapy for "anorexia" implies in their view that the problem to solve is "food" (Selvini Palazzoli, 1981; Selvini Palazzoli & Viaro, 1988). A therapist who accepts them for therapy implicitly does so in order to get rid of the so-called lack of appetite (anorexia). However, if the therapist openly or implicitly leads them to understand that she wants this self-starving member to eat, this in itself is sufficient to stimulate symmetry. The refusal of food is nothing but a symptom. It is neither the cause of the distress nor the real problem of the family. The more the therapist openly or implicitly pushes for change before working on the "family game," the less likely the change is to occur. One's attention must always be directed to the "game," regardless of the acuteness of the symptoms.

When families contact us about their problems regarding off-spring who are still in school, I always bear in mind that these children are at the intersection of *at least* five different subsystems: the parents-grandparents system, the parents-offspring system, the offspring system, the offspring-school system, and the offspring-age group system. Usually, parents tend to blame their child's problem on a sibling, on the school, or on a boy/girlfriend. These relations with their subsystems may indeed be difficult, but the symptoms in such cases are generally very light. If a therapist is faced with really severe relational disturbances, one must consider mainly the first three subsystems. When an "anorexic" starts refusing food in the wake of a failure at school, this failure may be taken as the un-clenching factor only if it has had notable repercussions at the level of family interactions.

I'll refer the reader to several articles (Selvini Palazzoli et al., 1980a; Selvini Palazzoli & Prata, 1982b; Selvini Palazzoli, 1985a) for a description of the most frequent traps the families set out for the therapist and the ways in which they can be avoided. A therapist must succeed in setting up the rules, explicitly or implicitly. If you obey those of the family, you become powerless to change the ongoing "game." There are families of veterans, pastmaster play-ers (the "chronic patients" as we call them) where the repetitive rules are so dangerous (Selvini Palazzoli, 1985a) that the therapist who obeys them risks clenching the "game" definitely in an un-breakable clamp. The I.P.'s response may be dramatic and cause an acute worsening of the symptoms, even leading to suicide or murder. These are the extreme "moves" the I.P. will resort to if, through ignorance or symmetry, the therapist leaves him/her with no honorable way to save face. The precept "Primum non nocere" (First don't harm) should be the first and foremost concern of a family therapist, particularly when the instrument used for intervention is powerful (Selvini Palazzoli & Prata, 1982a).

When the therapist's intervention is effectual, it brings about positive changes for the I.P. and other members of the family. The family's system will then signal on all levels, analogic and verbal, that it has been "freed." It is as though a cruel spotlight, focusing only on the "green table," the cards and the chips, were suddenly to vanish and the family awakes from a nightmare.

The systemic model probably has its shortcomings, but it appeals to me because it is dynamic and pragmatic, based as it is on "trial, error, and feedbacks." It can actually help change family "games." Every "error" is, of course, an attempt that has failed, but it also constitutes valuable information about what should not be done. It increases available information, helping to discard incorrect hypotheses and enabling one to choose accurate tools with which to intervene. Finally, the process becomes ever more precise, more finely tuned, more "ad hoc." There is no use repeating a "trial" that has proved an "error." This yields no new information and can only be a waste of precious time. The Latin adage "Errare humanum est, stultum est perseverare" ("To err is human, to persevere is stupid") is quite explicit and leaves no room for doubt.

In less severe cases, I use less powerful interventions than those of the New Method. This is, in fact, a difficult prescription to abide by. It implies great diligence and arouses a good deal of anxiety. Only parents who are required to face a severe array of symptoms every day will be sufficiently motivated to carry it out carefully, without cheating. Sometimes, the therapist will see what the "game" is, but will be unable to break it. Leaving the family unchanged is better than aggravating the situation through a wrong intervention, which may contribute to the ossification of a dysfunctional organization. For example, when the referring person is a prestigious sibling of the I.P., the therapist could make the "game" more ruthless by prescribing family therapy. The players may become more fierce and the I.P.'s state may worsen (Selvini Palazzoli, 1985a). The systemic therapist should not have a family model in mind. Trying to impose how a family ought to be smacks of omnipotence and has its roots in a moralistic attitude, arrogance, and symmetry. It only breeds trouble. One should be thankful if one succeeds in solving the stated family problem by setting them free from their "pathogenic game." Presuming that one can completely stop human beings from "playing" is tantamount to expecting them to turn into wax figures.

CONCLUDING REMARKS

Family therapy, which only developed during the sixties, is currently undergoing a highly crucial and delicate phase. Conceivably, it might be a case of growing pains, although the symptoms don't really conform to type. The crisis threatens to be a long and dangerous one. Here in Italy, where there has been a remarkable flowering of creative ingenuity in the field of family therapy, a dispirited attitude seems to be taking over. The danger is that Italian therapists may fall in with the modish American trend, as has happened before in a number of other situations. The most alarming consequence is that we appear to be scrapping all our painstakingly acquired knowledge of "family games." In fact, the genetic and organic theories which, hopefully, had definitely been put "out of business" by decades of research into living systems and their dynamics are back "on the market."

There is presently, in the United States, a strong tendency to revert to psychoanalytical thought, both in family and individual therapy. Occasionally, individual and family therapies are used jointly, which, from a systemic point of view, is pure nonsense. Why aren't the humanistic sciences blooming in America, the richest and most straightlaced country in the world? Why is that country not further ahead in the humanistic sciences and why does it seem to have problems getting the humanistic sciences off the ground? When it starts to take off, it lands again with a thud, failing to yield any enduring results.

One is led to think that in the land where "time is money" family therapy is seen as a business failure. Family therapists found out quickly that they were operating at a financial loss. Americans are resorting to less sophisticated instruments than family therapy, less time-consuming, less tiring, more tried, tested, and lucrative ones. These devices include an arsenal of psychotropic drugs, electroconvulsive therapy (ECT), leucotomy, and similar surgery. When I visited the U.S. in 1984, I was appalled by the persistent T.V. program endorsing the use of drugs, leucotomy, and ECT. The fashionable contrivances listed are all highly rewarding in the short run and successfully clamp a lid over a sewer of problems, bypassing the difficulties of actually resolving them. However, I wonder if our American colleagues might not discover that their chosen techniques will saddle them with their most dreaded bugaboo: a waste of time and money.

Truthfully, family therapy's only "value" lies in its contribution to the progress of the human sciences and its potential to correct dysfunctional relations. Investing in such an outlandish and extravagant long-term undertaking is apparently an option only "poor" European countries can afford to consider. Hopefully, we Europeans will not allow ourselves to be sidetracked from the sound direction we have chosen.

I have decided to proceed with the utmost caution and rigor, testing my data and weeding out hypotheses, theories, and methods that have shown themselves to be incorrect. My purpose is to provide valid explanations and working tools for those of my colleagues who do not share my privilege—a costly one, indeed—of being able to work in a private center for therapy and research, free from any type of constraint.

At present, my two cotherapists are Maria Vignato, Ph.D., and Luisa Bigoni Prata, Ph.D. My research associates are Cinzia Raffin and Susana Frondizi Bullrich.

2

The Telephone Chart

The Telephone Chart is "a cornerstone of the first interview with the family" (Di Blasio et al., 1986) because the information one gathers during a telephone interview is the basis used to formulate the initial hypothesis. A bureaucratic chart is perfectly useless because it doesn't provide a therapist with relational information.

This is my present standard chart, which takes only 20 to 30 minutes to complete:

Referring person: ⎯⎯⎯⎯⎯⎯⎯⎯⎯⎯⎯⎯⎯⎯⎯⎯⎯⎯⎯⎯⎯

Who called: ⎯⎯⎯⎯⎯⎯⎯⎯⎯⎯⎯⎯⎯⎯⎯⎯⎯⎯⎯⎯⎯⎯⎯

Initial diagnosis: (the diagnosis given by the caller) ⎯⎯⎯⎯⎯⎯

Place of residence: ⎯⎯⎯⎯⎯⎯⎯⎯⎯⎯⎯⎯⎯⎯⎯⎯⎯⎯⎯

Father: name, age, education, profession ⎯⎯⎯⎯⎯⎯⎯⎯⎯⎯

Mother: name, age, education, profession ⎯⎯⎯⎯⎯⎯⎯⎯⎯

Date of marriage: ⎯⎯⎯⎯⎯⎯⎯⎯⎯⎯⎯⎯⎯⎯⎯⎯⎯⎯⎯⎯

Religion: ⎯⎯⎯⎯⎯⎯⎯⎯⎯⎯⎯⎯⎯⎯⎯⎯⎯⎯⎯⎯⎯⎯⎯⎯⎯

Other members of the household and their relationship: ⎯⎯⎯⎯⎯

Children in order of birth: ⎯⎯⎯⎯⎯⎯⎯⎯⎯⎯⎯⎯⎯⎯⎯⎯

Name, age, education, profession: ⎯⎯⎯⎯⎯⎯⎯⎯⎯⎯⎯⎯⎯

Father's family: ⎯⎯⎯⎯⎯⎯⎯⎯⎯⎯⎯⎯⎯⎯⎯⎯⎯⎯⎯⎯⎯

Mother's family: _____

Problem: _____

Observations: _____

Information from the referring person: _____

Invited to the first session: _____

The Telephone Chart should be filled out by a member of the therapeutic team, thereby structuring from the very first contact a therapeutic context which leaves less margin for the family to maneuver.

Later, when the team meets for the *presession*, the therapist who made the chart may recall something not recorded. For example, the tone the person used when calling or the changes in the inflection of the voice when the person is talking about different members of the family. These and other deviations provide useful information.

The following was my report to the team about a mother who called because her son has a "persecution complex." At a certain moment, the mother told me: "Hold on for a moment!" Returning, she said: "My son is paranoid, you know, he always thinks that people are talking behind his back. So I just told him to wash his hair and closed him in the bathroom. Between the shampoo and the running water, he'll not hear our conversation." In this case, it is much too easy to make a connection between the symptoms of the I.P. and his mother's behavior.

A family playing "psychotic games" is often more subtle and covert than the one in the above case. For example, a father could say during our telephone conversation, "We withdrew our daughter from school during the last days of her school term because she thought her classmates were hatching plots against her. Once she was out of school, she began to relax." I don't ignore this offered information, but I wait until the session to examine the I.P.'s relationship with her teachers and classmates because I strongly doubt if anyone becomes "psychotic" due to school problems. The connection between the I.P. and the people involved must be vital and devastating to present "persecution ideas."

In my experience, patients follow the family's rules. They signal distress with their symptoms, while simultaneously camouflaging the fact of being deprived of love and esteem or of being so excluded from confidence that they feel their parents and siblings have formed a coalition against them. The I.P. alludes to something while simultaneously collaborating to keep the problem hidden. The caller must follow suit and maintain the camouflage of the ongoing relationship. When a caller speaks of "persecution ideas" centered around school or work, sooner or later we will find at home the Ariadne's thread weaving us across the family's relationships.

Another caller could report the I.P. believes someone is sending impulses to his legs, ordering them to move constantly backwards and forwards. This input would lead the team to hypothesize that a member of the family, usually the mother, is secretly giving a neuroleptic drug which provokes a discharge of unrestrainable impulses, obliging one to walk involuntarily. It is this relational information which is important when the team prepares the session's program.

HYPOTHESIS AND TELEPHONE-CHART HYPOTHESES

The items of the chart never vary but, as in a harmonium, we can press one of the notes longer than the others to get more information. It depends on what we are looking for. Thus, the Telephone Chart, which is used to hypothesize, is itself founded on hypotheses.

The moment the telephone conversation starts, certain resemblances to past cases come to mind and lead to probing in one direction rather than another.

The Problem of the Referring Person
(Selvini Palazzoli et al., 1980a)

Every family therapist has "good," "bad," and "impossible" referring persons in his/her casebook. The first group limit their mediation to suggesting the family meet with· the therapist. The second group will press the family into seeing the therapist and then refuse to let either the therapist or the family work in peace. One can invite the "bad" referring person to the first session.

However, this isn't always possible and in most cases serves no useful purpose. If I catch this "bad" referring person as I'm making out the telephone chart, I try to understand in what way he/she is involved in the family's "game." Immediately, I make every possible move to neutralize his/her influence and remove this player from the "gambling table," whether or not he/she is invited to the session. Often this person is instrumental in perpetuating the dysfunctional "game." However, in my professional career, I have invited the "bad" referring person to a session fewer than 10 times.

As for the "impossible" one, there is simply nothing one can do except tell the person who phones that the waiting list is booked solid for the next six months. One can also say: "I don't treat this type of case." I fully realize that it is very difficult for a new team to give this answer. In fact, it is much more difficult than for a long-established and renowned center. However, every team has the right to guard itself against the frustrations of failure. Remember, on final analysis it is the family who bears the brunt of the failure. If the referring person is "impossible" to deal with, I refuse the family. If that person is "good," I needn't invite him/her to the session.

1) The Rolling Family

This family will help me illustrate the approach one can use when dealing with a family "sent" by a "bad" referring person. In this example, the referring person was a university professor better known for his political maneuvering than for his skill as a physician. All the cases he referred bore his unmistakable mark: The people involved were invariably as arrogant and presumptuous as he was.

Mr. Rolling, a well-known surgeon, phoned the center concerning his daughter, Teresa, 18 years old, who was anorexic. I completed the chart and then told him that he would have to wait for some time because Dr. Selvini and I were busy at the moment. He tried to skip the waiting list in a very arrogant manner. I told him, in a strict tone, to phone next week for my answer. Immediately, he contacted Dr. Selvini, telling her that Professor T. had especially referred him and consequently he was sure that she could give him an appointment. Dr. Selvini referred him back to me.

Finally, he came to the center with his wife, an attractive woman 10 years younger than he, three tall handsome boys in their twenties, and their daughter. Teresa was a tall, ugly girl with a prominent nose, carrot-colored hair, tight jeans, and a shapeless sweater.

The family sat down, father and daughter close to each other on the left side of the room, one of the boys in the center of the row opposite to the mirror. Next to him sat the mother. On the right side of the room were the other two boys. I was the supervisor, Dr. Selvini the therapist. She tried desperately to get a response from the mother and/or from the children, passing quickly with her circular questioning from one to the other. They were all so reticent that Dr. Selvini was getting discouraged. I called her and told her that every time she asked the mother a question the three boys stretched their legs in unison, forming a protective barrier between her and the mother, while the anorexic girl kept pulling at her sweater. The only one trying to cooperate was the father.

Often the therapist is not aware, on a conscious level, of the analogic messages of the family. However, she/he is always affected and influenced by them on a deeper level. In this case, for example, Dr. Selvini was feeling completely rejected and left out.

During the discussion I had with her, we reviewed the unpleasant maneuvers of the father and also the telephone call of the mother: "My husband told me to phone today to be told the date you have set for our appointment." When I asked her if she had agreed to come, she repeated the same words, like an uninvolved secretary.

At this point, all the pieces of the puzzle began to fit together. We hypothesized that the entire family had been forced to come because of the father. Dr. Selvini went back to the family and, as planned, asked the least unfriendly boy to make a list, starting from the one most willing to come to the one least willing. Dr. Selvini's questions was direct and unexpected. The boy looked at his mother, who, with an almost imperceptible movement of her head, gave him permission to speak. The boy relaxed and gave Dr. Selvini the list she wanted: first his father, then himself and his brothers, his sister, and his mother last.

Everybody agreed to this rating, but now Mrs. Rolling wanted to explain her position. She had nothing against Dr. Selvini nor against helping her daughter, but she was angry because her husband had arranged everything with Professor T. and, as usual, she had only to obey. Dr. Selvini expressed her understanding in a humorous tone and the ice was immediately broken. Now everyone wanted to speak, since it was no longer "against mother" but "to help Teresa."

2) The Bersio Family

Referring person:	Dr. Perla, an acquaintance of Dr. Selvini. He was Mrs. Bersio's brother-in-law and had suggested family therapy because, in his opinion, Mrs. Bersio was responsible for his daughter Luisa.
Who called:	Dr. Perla's wife on *September 5, 1984.* She immediately started accusing her sister, Mrs. Bersio. I told her to have a member of the Bersio family phone since there was a chart to be completed with personal data. On *September 10, 1984,* Mrs. Bersio called. She seemed hasty and not motivated. Her daughter Luisa, age 21, five feet tall, weighing 64 pounds, had been anorexic for the past seven years. Dr. Perla is giving her an antidepressant (Anafranil three times a day).
Initial diagnosis:	Anorexia nervosa.
Place of residence:	Tradate.
Father:	Giano. Died in 1970, at the age of 42 in a car accident on Christmas Eve. Arts degree. Agent and travelling salesman in Lombardy.
Mother:	Wilma. Age 53. Secretarial courses. Employed until she married, then was

	a housewife. At Mr. Bersio's death, she started working as a baby-sitter.
Date of marriage:	February 10, 1962.
Religion:	Roman Catholic.
Other members of the household and their relationship:	The *maternal grandmother, Carolina*—age 80. The grandfather survived only a few months after Mrs. Bersio and her daughter moved there following Mr. Bersio's death.
Children in order of birth:	
Luisa	Age 21. Degree in languages. Taking French and English classes. She was seven when her father died.
Father's family:	*Father* died many years ago. *Mother* is in a nursing home. *A brother* died eight years ago in a car accident.
Mother's family:	*Father* died some years ago (1971). *Mother*, Carolina, age 80. A *sister*, Rosa, married to Dr. Perla. Two children.

Problem

Three years ago Luisa became amenorrheic. During her first year in college, she started refusing food and lost many pounds. She went through a battery of exams, including an E.E.G., which were all negative. She underwent individual therapy, which was a failure. For a while, Luisa lived at Dr. Perla's house, where she improved and, for some years, she weighed 88 pounds. Two years ago, she was hospitalized for two weeks because she was gaining weight and then rapidly losing it. Recently, Luisa had lost two pounds. She prepares her own food, which she eats only out of the house.

Mrs. Bersio has no idea of what pushed Luisa to start refusing food. Her teacher predicted Luisa would have great difficulties with her classmates, which she did, and Mrs. Bersio persuaded her to change her school. The entire family, nuclear and extended, is now focusing on Luisa's food. Mrs. Bersio has a good relationship with her sister, Rosa, and her brother-in-law. Luisa detests the Perlas, who are constantly trying to force-feed her. When she's home, Luisa usually eats in her room. Mrs. Bersio had already heard about Dr. Selvini and now Dr. Perla is suggesting that she come to the center.

Invited to the first session: Mrs. Bersio, Luisa, the maternal grandmother, and Mrs. Perla.

This case was a failure. The family game involving the referring person remained unchanged because his good credentials obscured the fact that he was not only *the* referring person and *the* physician of the I.P., but also *the* husband of the "prestigious sibling." But he had such impeccable credentials!

The Problem of the Sibling as the Referring Person
(Selvini Palazzoil, 1985a)

When the caller is a sibling of the I.P., the receiver should immediately prick up his ears and investigate if, as in Dr. Selvini's article, it is "the prestigious one" *on* and *with whom* the family has built such a game that family therapy cannot be done. The role he plays should be carefully investigated in the first and second session. It should be exposed, the players should be unmasked, and the entire situation redefined and reshaped.

The parents usually do not phone because, as the caller says, they are not motivated for family therapy, but he certainly is. He will say he is pushing his family to come mainly to help his poor tortured parents. In this case, it would be an easy task for the compiler of the chart to focus on the caller. However, the "prestigious sibling" could push one of his parents to phone the therapist and remain camouflaged.

In the Matta family, discussed below, it was the mother who called the Nuovo Centro in 1980, four years before Dr. Selvini and I discovered the "game" built on the I.P.'s sibling.

The "prestigious" Graziella remained so camouflaged that we didn't become aware of the "game" they were playing. Dr. Selvini and I prescribed family therapy and had to face a crushing failure.

In the case of the Sele family, the referring sibling was suspect because he was also a physician. However, he was not the "prestigious one." While completing the chart, we received some information concerning Mrs. Sele's sister, Ida.

At the end of the second session, when the "prestigious sibling" hypothesis had to be discarded, I therefore shifted to the "instigative game" hypothesis. It finally proved to be true. The parents were motivated and the therapy was successful.

In the Mina family, the referring person was a doctor, but the person who called for an appointment was a sibling. In this case, the "prestigious sibling" hypothesis proved to be true. Family therapy was refused and the concluding intervention was successfully based on the sibling.

1) The Matta Family

Referring person:	Dr. L., a neurologist.
Who called:	The mother, on February 4, 1980.
Initial diagnosis:	Schizophrenia.
Place of residence:	Genoa.
Father:	Lorenzo. Age 59, with primary school and vocational training. Self-employed. Two years ago he started working as a qualified electrician in a factory. He does not travel but is overworked and is rarely home.
Mother:	Zita. Age 49. Third year of high school. She kept the accounts and helped her husband while he was self-employed. A housewife.
Date of marriage:	January 5, 1952.
Religion:	Roman Catholic.

Other members of the
household and their
relationship: None.

Children in order of
birth:

Graziella Age 26, born in 1954. Secondary school. Secretarial training and employed as a secretary. In 1973 she married Marco, a psychology student. He was a nice boy, but "he studied too hard" and Graziella felt neglected. The whole Matta family was "hostile" because he married Graziella when she was "too young."

Graziella and Marco lived in an apartment above her parent's home, but the Matta family could not be contained. In order to save their marriage they moved to a flat nearby. However, they were financially dependent on Mr. Matta. Graziella dutifully went to visit her family every day. After five years of marriage, Marco and Graziella separated.

Graziella went back to the old apartment belonging to her parents and which they had left free. Now she is in a turbulent relationship with Giacomo, whom she refuses to marry because he's "too jealous." They live together, but in fits and starts. Mr. and Mrs. Matta disapprove of their affair. Graziella would like to visit her parents at lunch and dinner, but her brother makes terrible scenes and hits her.

Nico Age 24. He was in school till 13, then became a blue-collar worker until his

	military service. He has not worked since completing his military service.
Father's family:	Both parents are dead. He has a sister, living in Piedmont, married, with children. The Matta family has only a superficial contact with her.
Mother's family:	*Father* died many years ago. *Mother,* Marta, age 75, is ill but still lives in Genoa with her youngest son. Mrs. Matta visits her very often.

Problem

Nico started behaving "very nervously" when he was 16. He became engaged to Lia, a 16-year-old girl, and their relationship lasted for eight years. Lia left Nico five months ago due to a particularly violent scene of jealousy. Nico beat her and accused her of being his father's mistress. He was admitted to the hospital, where he stayed for 15 days. The diagnosis was "schizophrenia." In the hospital he met Dr. L., who prescribed his medication and sees him regularly. She said she was incapable of curing Nico and is willing to come to the center along with the family.

A few days ago, Nico began speaking to Dr. L., whereas previously he had refused to say a single word. Now he is beginning to communicate with his mother, albeit through gestures. He's very solitary, stays in bed, and doesn't cause any trouble. Mrs. Matta would like to work, but she can't because of Nico. There is a conflict between Mr. and Mrs. Matta. The wife reproaches her husband for being more interested in his work than in his family. The only person Mrs. Matta can talk with is Graziella.

Invited to the first session: the nuclear family and Dr. L. (who didn't come). Nico, the "victim of the game," created smoke screens, hiding his hatred for Graziella behind "a crazy jealousy" for Lia.

This case was a failure because we were not aware of two major problems: "The Problem of the Referring Person" combined with that of "A Sibling as the Referring Person."

2) The Sele Family

Referring person:	Prof. C., who only knows the I.P.'s brother, Gino, an M.D.
Who called:	Gino, on May 13, 1985, for his sister, Maria, a 30-year-old "manic depressive." Troubles had begun five years ago. Several admissions to hospitals plus abortive attempts at individual and group therapy. She is depressed, at present, and takes antidepressants. The parents don't call by themselves because, "unfortunately," anything in the medical line is always left to Gino even though he no longer resides in the family's home.
Initial diagnosis:	Manic-depressive psychosis.
Place of residence:	Ravenna.
Father:	Gennaro. Age 62, architect, retired two years ago. Private professional income and a pension. He comes from Alberobello in the south of Italy.
Mother:	Valeria. Age 61, majored in foreign languages, formerly taught French in high school. Retired three years ago because she was in poor health.
Date of marriage:	November 5,1952.
Religion:	Roman Catholic.
Other members of the household and their relationship:	None.
Children in order of birth:	
Gino	Age 31 (January 15, 1954). In 1973 he went to Bologna to study and became a medical doctor working in a

hospital with a private practice. Married Alma in 1977. Separated in 1982. His daughter, Silvia, age 4½, lives with him. The separation was by mutual consent. He has the custody of the child. He left his parents' home when he was 20 years old and has lived on his own since.

Maria   Age 30. Degree in natural sciences. Has held temporary stand-in teaching jobs in and around Ravenna in 1984–1985. Debilitating bouts of depression in January and February. At present, she rejects any occasional offers to teach. Never officially engaged, but she had a particular relationship with *Franco,* a chronically unemployed worker.

Carla   Age 26. Majored in foreign languages. At present not involved with anyone. She is looking for a job.

Bianca   Age 18. In her third year of high school, good student. She has a boyfriend.

Father's family: *Father* died when Gennaro was 17. *Mother* died eight years ago. A *sister* died 10 years ago. A *brother* living in Argentina.

Mother's family: *Father* died in 1972. *Mother* in 1981. A *brother,* married with children, lives in Bologna. An unmarried *sister,* Ida, lives in Bologna and is very much involved in Valeria's family affairs.

Problem

During the spring of 1980, Maria had her first crisis. She was a brilliant student but did not complete her final exam. Episodes of unhappy love affairs would lead her to quit her studies. She alternates between periods of euphoria and depression. When she feels distressed, she stays in bed for days on end. Antidepressants had her weighing as much as 176 pounds two years ago. In 1983, she stopped medication and started individual analysis, followed by psychotherapy at the hospital.

Her individual analysis was rather dramatic because it caused her severe anguish. At present she insists that she must cope with her problems without outside help. Actually, she spends all day in bed staring. The situation is getting out of hand because she is threatening to commit suicide. After two fierce quarrels with her father, Maria took a great quantity of antidepressants and her stomach had to be pumped. Maria claims life is "revolting." Gino has been "roped back in" because of "all of that." He told her she isn't really ill and he suggested coming to my center. Maria is willing to.

Gino left home when he was 20 because the atmosphere was stifling. Mrs. Sele was overprotective. Both parents were domineering and exerted undue restrictions. Besides, Ravenna is a "stultifying" place to live in. He left as soon as he was enrolled at Bologna University. He started working and living with his wife-to-be, much to his family's disapproval. Then he married her, fathered a daughter, and separated, despite his parents' disapproval. His sisters see him as a "prestigious figure," the one who managed to leave home. He visits his family roughly once a month without particular problems. The parents view him as "the one who knows how to get by." Questioned by Dr. Prata, Gino says he read the word "prestigious figure" in the *Pragmatics of Human Communication* by Watzlawick, Beavin, and Jackson (1967). This information is not correct. Has he heard something about "A Sibling as the Referring Person" (1985a) by Dr. M. Selvini Palazzoli?

3) The Mina Family

Referring person:	Dr. X, psychiatrist who is giving drugs to the I.P.
Who called:	Carla, in June 1985, for her brother Ciro, 23 years old.

Initial diagnosis:	Actually, it's not clear if Ciro is depressed or schizophrenic like his father.
Place of residence:	Lecco.
Father:	Elio. Age 62. No proper schooling after the first grade. Self-taught. Worked four years for a magazine, then was fired because he was feeling persecuted. Diagnosed as a paranoid schizophrenic and for many years under medical supervision. He is a severe, raving paranoid, with delusions of grandeur and of persecution: television and mass media are under his control. Daily, they speak about him. Physically, he is very healthy. The city council gave him a disability pension and an apartment. After their divorce, Mr. Mina maintained their relationship. He has no living members in his family of origin.
Mother:	Attila. Age 61, she has a master's degree in philosophy. Worked all her life as a schoolteacher to support her four children. Retired in June 1985.
Date of marriage:	May 11, 1952, when Mrs. Mina was six months pregnant. She ran away from her family home after a violent dispute. Her family disapproved of her pregnancy and her engagement to Mr. Mina. A few months later, they married. Both were born in Southern Italy.
Legal separation:	1965.
Divorce:	1978.

Mrs. Mina's second marriage:	1979 to Mr. V., an old wartime flame. He was twice widowed, has a 25-year-old *daughter.* He courted Mrs. Mina tirelessly and she finally married him. His apartment was close to theirs and Mrs. Mina kept running from one apartment to the other, devoting herself to Mr. V. and the children.
Mrs. Mina's 2nd legal separation:	1982. Mr. V. was opposed to the separation. For revenge, he walked out with all Mrs. Mina's belongings. It's been a very grim affair.
Religion:	Roman Catholic.
Other members of the household and their relationship:	None.
Children in order of birth:	
Carla	Age 34. Several attempts at obtaining a university degree. She cannot study because she has to take care of Ciro. Taught grade school until June 1984, when she retired. Married in June 1982, to *Aldo*, age 57, architect. They have no children. Carla would like to become a writer.
Anna	Age 30. Second-grade schoolteacher. She lives alone, 50 yards away from her family's house.
Marco	Age 27. He is getting a degree in economics. He is extremely anxious about Ciro and therefore has trouble concentrating on his studies. Has never had a girlfriend.

Ciro Age 23. During his second year in high school he flunked out and appealed to the legal authorities, claiming an unfair procedure. Mrs. Mina and Carla supported him, believing he had been treated unfairly. He was readmitted to school, but the teachers harassed him badly and forced him to quit.

Father's family: *Father* died after emigrating to Mexico. *Mother* died when Mr. Mina was five. He was brought up by his paternal grandparents. A younger *sister* died many years ago.

Mother's family: *Father* died in 1955. *Mother* died 12 years ago when she was 82. Three *sisters* and two *stepsisters*. They never see each other.

Problem

Ciro became deaf when he was three years old, but continued to speak normally. After failing in school, he started taking Valium and hashish. This made him sleep during the day and stay awake all night. After being admitted to hospitals three times (the last in June 1984), he stopped taking drugs. He is in great distress, afraid of everything, refuses to leave the house, and "feels responsible for all the troubles in the universe." He sleeps very little and badly, staying in bed until late in the day; then he gets up, but does nothing at all. He hardly speaks to his family.

When Carla told him she had found in a book the address of a center for family therapy, Ciro appeared to be willing to come. Anyway, Carla and Mrs. Mina have succeeded in convincing him to accept therapy. Carla plays a paternal role in the family. Her husband, Aldo, takes part in tackling Ciro's problems. Six months ago, having decided that Mrs. Mina was "pathogenic," Carla and her husband invited Ciro to live with them. And he accepted.

Invited to the first session: Mrs. Mina, the children, and Aldo. Mr. Mina apparently can't be invited because he doesn't live with the family and doesn't want to talk about problems. He gets upset easily and feels persecuted. Besides, Ciro refuses to see him and refuses to attend the session if his father is there.

The "Germ Barrier"
(Prata, 1989)

My hypothesis regarding the "phobia of dirt" is that the identified patient constructs a "germ barrier" to retain someone inside the nuclear family and keep out a member of the extended family.

In my experience, the so-called "fear of microbes" is more frequently found in young women who, as a result of their marriage or the birth of a child, had to give up their studies or work. Usually, they are particularly dynamic and ambitious women, while their husbands are more of the flabby, spineless, and sluggish varieties. These amicable men are often well liked by their work colleagues but much less esteemed by their bosses, who consider them lazy and slackers. They maneuver to be underachievers and are frustrating to their wives because of their economic and social failures.

The vicious circle begins. The more the wife pushes, the more the husband becomes passive. Nothing can make him react or answer back because he never gets angry. Generally, this man has either a mother or an older sister who commands absolute obedience. He also behaves in an overly dutiful manner towards his wife, only to drop her immediately whenever a member of his own family sends out a signal. The scales will not even tip in the wife's favor after the birth of a child. The family of origin always comes first. The husband continues to behave more as a dutiful, irreproachable son than a husband. In fact, by not raising a finger to stop his mother from interfering with his child's upbringing, he will sorely undermine his wife's authority.

Daily, the wife becomes more frustrated, discredited, and gets furious. However, her outbursts of rage have no effect on him. Possibly, this wife may have gone through a stage of "obsessive rituals" in her own adolescence. Investigating the rapport she had with her mother, we will discover it was strained and difficult with an asphyxiating type of mother. The daughter had successfully used the "obsessive rituals" to keep her at bay.

To get rid of her overly intrusive mother, she married a sweet, loving, absolutely noninterfering man, hoping to have him as an ally against her. On the contrary, her kind and helpful husband immediately won his mother-in-law over. Now, the latter can count on a strong ally, which affords her free access to her daughter's private life.

At this point, "inexplicably" the young wife starts fearing dirt, washing herself, disinfecting the house and everyone coming into it. "The green table" is ready; all the gamblers are there and extremely well trained. One can easily see why a young wife might resort to a "germ barrier," both in self-defense and to regain the upper hand. The move, whether of recent design or tried and tested, tends to be successful for some time. Many calls go through the "barrier," but everyone remains in everyone's home. The husband, performing his role of the long-suffering complier, will simply dodge taking an active part. He will not even protect his children from the constant washings and disinfectings their mother inflicts on them. The children, obeying the rules of the family "game," don't rebel openly; they complain but submit. Sometimes, during primary school or preadolescence, they can develop some mild symptoms, like laziness in studying, some loss of appetite, excessive slowness during meals, a slight increase in weight, nocturnal enuresis, and so on.

It is usually the I.P. herself who calls for family therapy and provides the data for the telephone chart (Di Blasio et al., 1986). At the end of the conversation, if I ask her which member of the extended family she thinks we should invite to the first session, she either says she doesn't want anyone to come or chooses her mother. Since seeing a couple alone provides the therapist with very little information on the family "game," I'm obliged to invite all the members of the household, plus one or two members of the extended family. One must choose whom to invite: the family of the husband *or* the family of the wife (Di Blasio et al., 1986). It doesn't help to work with anyone the I.P. opposes strongly. If one does, the session only ends with everyone being distrustful and no one willing to discuss anything meaningful. In the presence of that unwanted person, the basic rule is: "Silence! The enemy is listening to you!"

During the first telephone conversation, I try to discover whom the "germ barrier" may have been set up against. Then, during the first or the second session, I ask the I.P. point-blank: "Mrs. XX, who is it you are trying to keep out of your home and family with this "germ barrier"?

This question never fails to produce an amazement, a loosening of tension, and finally a nice, hearty laugh. "Tell me, Mrs. XX, does the barrier work?" A name will always be forthcoming. This is the person she started the escalation against since she was not able to confine her husband. She wants him for herself and she would like him to assume a less wishy-washy attitude and be "more of a man." He should be more competitive, more of a "go-getter" in his job, so that he can give her the social status she craves.

Obviously, clarifying this point and the function of the "germ barrier" is not enough to change the rules of the "game." Now, family therapy can give the couple alternative instruments to get out of the "game." Most of the cases I've dealt with directly or as a supervisor using the New Method had a positive effect on all members of the nuclear family.

In fact, the New Method introduces reorganizing information into the family which compels them to mark out the limits and separate the roles, thus creating less disturbed and disturbing channels of communication.

1) The G.B. Family

Referring person:	Mrs. G.B. (the I.P.)
Who called:	Mrs. G.B.
Initial diagnosis:	"Fear of germs" (Rupophobia)
Place of residence:	Milan
Father:	Adriano. Age 29, born in R., a little town near Bari (Southern Italy). Secondary school, vocational training. He teaches draftmanship. He does not travel for his work.

Mother:	**Valeria** (Mrs. G.B.). Age 23. She completed three years of psychology at the University of Milan before quitting her studies when she got pregnant. She, too, comes from R. She and her husband met in Milan. They went to their small hometown for their wedding and then settled in Milan permanently.
Date of marriage:	January 2, 1978. Mrs. G.B. was pregnant at the time.
Other members of the household and their relationship:	None.
Children in order of birth:	
Flavia	Age 18 months. She is well and healthy.
Father's family:	*Father,* Natale. Age 65. *Mother,* Assunta. Age 55. Live near Bari and are in good health. There is a *sister,* Camilla, 32, married to a truck driver, Giacomo, who is frequently out of town. They live in Milan and had *triplets* in 1978. After their birth, Camilla moved to her mother's home for six months and gave up her flat to the G.B.s. When she returned, she moved into a flat in the same building.
Camilla is illiterate, unintelligent, and has very old-fashioned views. She relies heavily on Mr. G.B. Every time she comes to visit, with her three children in tow, Mrs. G.B. has nightmares about the perils of germ infections. Mr. G.B. is very attached to Camilla and goes to see her two or three times

a day, either by himself or with Flavia. Camilla, due to her triplets, managed to enlist Mr. G.B. as well as the rest of her family of origin in helping her with everything.

Mother's family: *Father,* Ciro. Age 60. *Mother,* Caterina. Age 50. There is *an older sister* who is married and *a younger one* still living with her parents. They all live near Bari. Her father, although he didn't know about her pregnancy, wept for two months at having to part from her when Mrs. G.B. married.

Problem

Mrs. G.B. suffers from severe anxiety, which has been increasing steadily. She lives by a system of very strict rules, which she is forced to obey. Any transgression throws her into a state of panic. She has to do all her laundry twice and then disinfect it before she irons it. This means that the dirty laundry has piled up and Mr. G.B. can never find anything clean to wear.

In addition, before Mrs. G.B. can throw her plastic garbage bags away she has to empty out their contents and inspect them, not once but twice. Although this is one of her self-imposed mandatory injunctions, she is always so tired that she can't get around to doing it in time. The plastic garbage bags, therefore, are piled up in the hallway smelling. There are eight of these foul sacks cluttering up their hallway at present. There is not much room to move around anymore.

Mrs. G.B. had ritual obsessions when she was 15: for instance, she insisted on her mother saying "Good night" 15 times before she would agree to go to bed. Then, getting married has made her life all the more complicated, given that she has more responsibilities now then ever before. Her family never comes to visit; if they did, she'd be terrified of the microbes they might bring along with them. Mrs. G.B. never goes to visit Camilla.

As for Mr. G.B., he is very worried because his wife's anxiety

has steadily increased since last November and has now reached
an alarming level. Their family doctor has prescribed tran-
quillizers, but Mrs. G.B. won't take them. She's afraid they'll
make her symptoms disappear: she wants to come to the center
with all her symptoms in full bloom. Mrs. G.B. got pregnant in
November 1977, which is also when her first symptom appeared.
Mr. G.B. does all the household chores and also helps her disinfect the laundry and inspect the garbage, although to no avail.
Mrs. G.B. doesn't trust anyone to accomplish these tasks properly.
Mr. G.B., with all the help Camilla requires constantly from him
and everything Mrs. G.B. needs him to do around the house, never
has a minute to himself and can't even find time to prepare his
school lectures. However, he never complains. *Remarks:* This family was referred to me and the phone call was made to my residence. It was 11 P.M. and I could hear a child running around. So
I asked Mrs. G.B. if the child was always up that late. Mrs. G.B.
replied that Flavia did this only when she (Mrs. G.B.) was especially upset. She said her husband disagreed with Flavia's staying
up so late, but accepted the fact that it happened (and she
laughed!).

Invited to the first session: the nuclear family unit, plus Camilla
and Giacomo. Mrs. G.B. immediately says that Camilla interferes
in their lives and that she would not feel free to speak out if
Camilla were present. As for Giacomo, Mrs. G.B. says he's always
away. I make an exception and agree to meet the nuclear family
only.
   When the G.B. family arrived at the center, I was struck by their
appearance. Mrs. G.B. was a very attractive, well made-up, slim,
carefully coiffed, and simply but elegantly dressed woman. Flavia
was a charming little girl, dressed in a nice embroidered dress with
a pink sweater. She held tightly to her father's hand. Mr. G.B. was
a young man of 29, looking 35, overweight with a potbelly, wearing
blue jeans, a shirt of indefinite color, and torn tennis shoes, which
were certainly not making him look smarter. He fell into a chair as
if he was an extremely tired or indolent man. He gave the impression that if I pricked him he would deflate like a life-sized rubber

dummy. He was slow-witted and sluggish in his thoughts and speech.

Contrarily, Mrs. G.B. was smart, quick in understanding, and ready with appropriate answers. They were both cooperating, but Mr. G.B. was so slow that he tempted one's patience to an extreme. I often had to intervene to prevent Mrs. G.B. from answering for him. He showed himself to be willing to cooperate, but answered more and more slowly. Mrs. G.B., visibly irritated, wanted to intervene and take the initiative. I was running the risk of obeying the rules of the family "game." This consisted of discouraging me from addressing Mr. G.B. and inducing me to choose Mrs. G.B. as the privileged interlocutor. Fortunately, I became aware of their tactic and tried consistently to bring him out and avoid being "seduced" by her.

On the whole they were a "simpatico" couple: Mr. G.B. seemed to be the classic stereotype of men from Southern Italy at the mercy of a frenetic "Milanese" woman. But the situation could be seen in the opposite way: a frenetic Milanese at the mercy of a sweet and passive man from the South. However, they were both from the same little town, and it was evident that Mr. G.B.'s passivity and Mrs. G.B.'s activity were only reciprocally provocative behaviors.

At one point, as Mr. G.B. was describing his "martyrdom"—all his wife's prohibitions and his own renunciations—I asked him to give me an example of a prohibition he had been subjected to. He replied, with a very sad voice, that for more than a year now he couldn't take down from a cupboard a miniature ship he had started making with the greatest enthusiasm. His slightest allusion to this ship would provoke a panic in his wife because of "all the germs aboard!" Mr. G.B. looked visibly frustrated. Suddenly, Mrs. G.B. burst out laughing, but immediately tried to check herself by covering her mouth with a hand. I picked up this reaction without any comment. I mentally linked it to an analogous reaction Mrs. G.B. had when, filling out the telephone chart, she told me her husband disagreed with Flavia going to bed at midnight, but finally had resigned himself. Then she burst out laughing.

These pieces of information confirmed my impression that her "condition" was less "serious" than it seemed to be and that her behavior had a precise aim. The problem was to uncover the motive. Ending the first session, I said I needed more data to make a decision and enlisted Camilla and Giacomo to help me. Mr. and Mrs. G.B. agreed to invite them. So Camilla and Giacomo came to the second session. With the information provided by Camilla, I knew Mr. G.B. also played the martyr with her. Naturally, it so happened that Camilla had a "phobia"! Before meeting Giacomo, her parents had sent her to Milan to care for Adriano (Mr. G.B.) In a short time she had a "fear of thieves." She absolutely couldn't remain at home alone because she would become terrified! Adriano would immediately return home after school. He was "sacrificing" himself and could never ever go out in the evening. When he absolutely needed to go to Bari to visit Valeria, during his university's vacations, he performed a gruelling tour de force by going and returning in two days (Valeria probably never forgave him for that!).

In response to my question, Camilla said she was surprised to see that Adriano had no reaction, not even a complaint, for all of the problems she had created for him during his student years at school. At present, she couldn't understand her brother's acceptance of his wife pretentions (of which she knew only a hundredth part). He didn't shirk from her own demands, although with her it was certainly different "because she had triplets"! Addressing Camilla and Valeria, I said that, in my opinion, they were engaged in a fierce competition. They wanted to see which one would succeed in exasperating Adriano to the point of making him react and scream, "Stop it!" However, they were far from achieving their goal.

Camilla did not seem to understand; Mr. G.B., as usual, didn't react and Mrs. G.B. sent me a mischievous look. I sent Camilla and Giacomo to the waiting room and made the "testing of motivations and expectations" with the nuclear family present. I declared family therapy advisable and invited only Mr. and Mrs. G.B. to the third session. Then we gave the *secret*. Later we prescribed *the evening disappearances*.

Before proceeding with the "New Method," I asked Mr. G.B. to take over the household entirely. I told Mrs. G.B. to heed all of Camilla's calls for help. Thus, Mr. G.B. was able, through our prescription, without having suggested anything specific, to get rid

of all the piled-up garbage bags and to take the heaps of dirty
clothes to the laundry. As for Camilla, when she summoned Mr.
G.B. and found herself confronted with a smiling Mrs. G.B. willing to do anything for her, she stopped asking for help. She started
caring for her own household and relied a lot more on her husband,
who was overjoyed by this turn of events and decided to return to
Bari. Family therapy was interrupted after the ninth session, leaving one session in the "reserve fund."

Three years later,* the follow-up displayed a positive evolution
for all family members.

2) The Casta family

Referring person:	Dr. B. who had performed a series of hypnotic sessions with negative results.
Who called:	Mrs. Casta, the I.P., on September 3, 1984, for her "fear of germs and dirt." Five days earlier, she had attempted suicide with sleeping pills and was in a coma for a day.
Initial diagnosis:	"Fear of germs and dirt" (rupophobia).
Place of residence:	Genoa.
Father:	Vittorio. Age 36. Secondary school, electrical technician. Working on night shifts as a city policeman. Doesn't travel.
Mother:	**Lisa.** (Mrs. Casta). Age 32. Trained as an accountant. Has worked since she was 18. After her second pregnancy, started working part time.
Date of marriage:	August 10, 1975.
Religion:	Roman Catholic.

*In 1980, we used to undertake a follow-up procedure three years after the last session.
Now, following Bebe Speed's suggestion (1985), we do it after six months.

Other members of the household and their relationship:	None

Children in order of birth:

Silvia	Age 7 (born on May 22, 1977). Second grade. Good student. Enuresis during the night.
Sabrina	Age 2½. She attends nursery school.
Father's family:	*Father*, Ettore. Age 60. *Mother*, Elena. Age 63. They live nearby and disapprove of Mrs. Casta's way of educating Silvia and Sabrina. This disagreement created a gap between Mrs. Casta and her in-laws. They are estranged. She has a married *sister* living in Bergamo and an unmarried *brother* living with her parents.
Mother's family:	*Father*, Achille. Age 70. Has Alzheimer's disease and sleeps all day. *Mother*, Rina. Age 60. They live five minutes away from the Castas' home. He has a *sister*, married, with a son, very attached to Mrs. Casta. They live in Milan but visit very seldom.

Problem

Mrs. Casta feels confused. Her main problem concerns cleanliness. Her home is hallowed ground. Mr. Casta has to wash himself frequently. The girls, in particular, must undergo continuous washings and scrubbings by their mother. Her fear of germs has become critical over the years, especially after the second pregnancy.

In addition, Mrs. Casta keeps her husband home because she's afraid to stay alone with her two small children. She doesn't know whether the fear is for herself or them. She had never felt any urge to harm them. Mrs. Casta's mother has always been very concerned about her and has become extremely anxious even since her suicide attempt. Mrs. Casta says she took those sleeping pills because her husband had chosen to go to work and left her home. In the hospital, and then at home, her mother and Mr. Casta took turns caring for her. Now, they constantly watch her because they're afraid she might attempt suicide again. She doesn't think she will. Both Mrs. and Mr. Casta are very eager to resolve this fear of germs, which has persisted for years.

Invited to the first session: the nuclear family and Mrs. Casta's mother.

Mrs. Casta was a slim, nice-looking woman, dressed with care. Mr. Casta was a heavy, bald-headed man, poorly dressed. The older daughter, Silvia, was a plump, passive girl. When I asked Mrs. Casta: "Madam, against whom, mainly, did you build this 'germ barrier,' " she looked at me with a mischievous eye, then laughed and replied: "Against my mother-in-law!" She then listed a number of malicious remarks her mother-in-law had made against her since they got married and even more so after Sabrina's birth. Mr. Casta has never said a word or done anything to protect her. Contrary to his wife's wishes, he goes daily to see his parents, taking their children with him. Mr. Casta said he never pays attention to his mother's criticisms of his wife. He goes there only to help them. He also helps his wife in the house.

Before ending the session, I decided to give a "systemic jolt" to Silvia. "My poor darling, you are such a silly girl! You let your mother wash and dry you up like a handkerchief at your age! The only protest you're able to raise is to make your mother clean you in the evening when she no longer wants to!" The plump Silvia stopped lounging and became furiously erect in the chair. At our next session, I discovered she had stopped her enuresis.

Then came Mr. and Mrs. Casta's turn to receive a "jolt." I called Mr. Casta his wife's "little slave" and a "real sheep" because he didn't protect his children from being summoned home at 5:00 P.M. and scrubbed until dinnertime. Turning to Mrs. Casta, I said, "The real jackass is you." She never had the courage to revolt against her mother's intrusiveness and now she has built this "germ barrier" to keep her mother-in-law out and her husband in, instead of expressing herself clearly! Mr. and Mrs. Casta said I was right, then everyone relaxed and smiled.

The team decided that family therapy was needed. The parents were invited to the third session, but not the two girls.

The New Method proved successful. Silvia became more autonomous and determined. Mrs. Casta's confusion, anxiety, and "germ barrier" rapidly disappeared. Mr. Casta remained in the police corps, obtaining a better position and a higher income.

The relationships between the members of the family developed more satisfactorily. We interrupted therapy at the sixth session. We advised Mr. and Mrs. Casta to keep the *secret* also that therapy had been interrupted. This was a decision involving only the three of us. They still had in the "reserve fund" four sessions, which they could utilize if necessary. I asked them to contact me after six months to tell me how things were going. They did. Everything in the family was fine and they were moving to a new house.

The analogic message contained in the symptom "fear of dirt" is, under certain aspects, surprisingly explicit. Take the first example. How could we really believe that this mischievous Mrs. G.B. is actually afraid of dirt? Then we could never explain why she fills her home's entrance with smelly bags of garbage. We must ask ourselves: What pushed and still pushes her to act in this apparently contradictory way? What is the pragmatic effect of her behavior? We know that nobody can walk in or out of the G.B.s' home without stumbling over a wall of garbage. So we ask: Who is the person that the identified patient does not want to let into the house and who is the person that the identified patient does not want to let out of the house?

To get the appropriate answer, one usually should quickly go through the description of the symptoms and shift the investigation to the tale of the family and the story of the identified patient *in* the family. Then we reach the crux of the problem and discover contorted relations, interferences, undue intrusions, and frustrated expectations which provoked disorder, hierarchical confusion, grudges, and longing for a return match or revenge.

At this point, if we want to be efficacious, we have to break open the dysfunctional "game" by intervening systemically on those relationships and introducing a new homeostasis.

In the cases I have treated, the New Method has proved particularly effective.

The "Withdrawal of Significant Ones"
(Prata, 1988)

The subject of this section is depression, which, in the last decades, has become a major social problem. Books and articles on depression are so numerous that an extensive literature survey would be exhausting. When one member of a couple is showing symptoms of depression or anorexia nervosa, my hypothesis is that the other member of the couple has "stolen" all the "significant ones" from the I.P.

The Bar Family

Mr. Bar had progressively won over to himself his in-laws and his two little daughters. When Mrs. Bar started her second pregnancy, she hoped the new baby would belong entirely to her and compensate for all the withdrawal pangs she had already suffered. Instead, as her pregnancy advanced, she concluded that her husband would "steal" the second baby as well. She became "depressed." This move didn't change anything in the family dynamics. She doubled the stakes and became "anorexic." The results backfired. Mrs. Bar was becoming seriously emaciated when they phoned the center.

When the family arrived, we found that Mr. Bar was a tall and very handsome man, while Mrs. Bar, who had certainly been a pretty little woman, had become a pale skeleton.

Referring person:	Dr. Teli, Mr. Bar's colleague in the same private clinic.
Who calls:	Mr. Bar, on September 9, 1986, for his wife's anorexia nervosa.
Initial diagnosis:	Anorexia nervosa.
Place of residence:	Como.
Religion:	Roman Catholic.

Father:	Santo. Age 36. M.D. in a private clinic in Como. He doesn't travel for work.
Mother:	**Erica,** (Mrs. Bar). Age 29. Upper high school graduate, has never worked. She got married at the age of 20 and has always been a housewife.
Date of marriage:	September 8, 1977.
Other members of the household and their relationship:	None. Mrs. Bar's parents live close by.
Children in order of birth:	
Maria	Age 8, born July 5, 1978. Third grade. She's a good student.
Giuliana	Age 5. She's in kindergarten and enjoys it.
Father's family:	*Father,* Bernardo. Age 71. *Mother,* Bruna. Age 61. They live in Como, but spend eight months a year in Umbria. They're often together with the Bars. An elder brother, Giaco, is divorced and has a daughter, Giudi.
Mother's family:	*Father,* Marco. Age 57. He has land with greenhouses and hothouses. *Mother,* Emi. Age 55. Emi had breast cancer four years ago. At present she seems in good health. *A sister,* Lella, who is single and lives with her parents. Engaged to Roberto. The grandparents look after Maria and Giuliana whenever Mr. and Mrs. Bar are out. The two families meet daily.

Problem

Five years ago, during her second pregnancy, Mrs. Bar began losing weight and never resumed menstruating after this pregnancy. She is five and a half feet tall and weights 88 pounds. She refuses food, presents bouts of bulimia and induced vomiting, and occasionally takes laxatives. Mr. Bar thinks she takes more laxatives than she admits. Mrs. Bar underwent individual therapy with a psychologist several times a week but refused to communicate with her. So it was unsuccessful. Mr. Bar doesn't trust his wife and controls her closely. The children have a good relationship with their mother, although she does not have a warm, outgoing personality. Mrs. Bar is aloof, but very dynamic.

At this point I ask Mr. Bar if Mrs. Bar is at home and if I could speak directly to her. Mrs. Bar says she is aware of the seriousness of her problem. Actually, she would have called today. The fact that Family Therapy has been suggested by Mr. Bar's friend and colleague doesn't bother her.

Invited to the first session: the nuclear family, Mrs. Bar's parents, and her sister Lella.

Second Part of the First Session—September 20, 1986

Spontaneous seating arrangement:

Giuliana °	Maria °	°Grandfather
Mr. Bar °		°Lella
Mrs. Bar °		°Grandmother
	Dr. Prata °	

———————————————————————

Mirror

(I was testing the affective "Withdrawal of Significant Ones" hypothesis and Mrs. Bar's hunger strike effectiveness.)

Dr. Prata: Mrs. Bar were you able to become a real wife through your hunger strike? Did you succeed? How do you feel? You were *the daughter* and you hoped you'd become a wife.

Mrs. Bar: I feel more like a daughter than a wife.

Dr. Prata: What about the fantasy of being a mother? That's not
            even in the picture! This family has so many mothers
            and they are all better than you. Aren't they? You
            are only seen as a daughter. . . .

Mrs. Bar: Right. A daughter who needs everyone's help all the
            time.

Dr. Prata: You never get credit for being Maria and Giuliana's
            mother, do you?

Mrs. Bar: I never do. I have all these people around giving me
            advice. No one lets me make my own mistakes!
            Whenever I make a decision, someone always pipes
            up and says: "Oh, no, you are wrong, *this* is the best
            way to do that." The children no longer come and
            ask me: "Mom, can we do this?" When they come
            and I say no, they ask Grandma and what she says is
            right.

Dr. Prata: We have a serious confusion in the hierarchy.

Mrs. Bar: Right. I don't known. Maybe not in the hierarchy.

Dr. Prata: Yes, Madam! And hierarchy is very important. If an
            apprentice gardener, who's just been hired, were to
            go and tell your father what he must do, your father
            would immediately put him in his place, wouldn't
            he? He'd say: "Look, I'm the boss and you're the
            smallest cog in the whell. Shut up!" Hierarchy,
            whether in a business or in a family, is very impor-
            tant. In this particular family, you have ended up as
            Maria and Giuliana's little sister!

Mrs. Bar: Yes, that's exactly how I feel. I can't even tell what
            is wrong anymore, even in the most trivial matters. I
            actually feel relieved when my parents decide, or
            even my children. If Maria says: "Let's do it this
            way," I answer: "Good, we'll do that." It's the same
            with the rest of the family.

Dr. Prata: The children have become your big sisters.

Mrs. Bar: Yes.

Dr. Prata: Are you thinking of having another child, hoping to become a real mother to him?

Mrs. Bar: No, I don't think so.

Dr. Prata: "If I give birth to four kids one of them might think of me as their mother." Have you given up trying?

Mrs. Bar: Yes, I have.

Dr. Prata: To the extent of turning off the menstruation tap, to rule out the idea of having any more children for the time being?

Mrs. Bar: Right.

Dr. Prata: Mrs. Bar, have you even come out with a verbal protest? Have you even tried to rebel? You're doing a banal hunger strike; it is a hunger strike without any explanation. In Ireland, Bobby Shands and ten companions who starved to death said: *"We're going on a hunger strike because we want you, England, to acknowledge our rights as political prisoners."* They all starved to death after a hunger strike with a declared purpose.

Here we are dealing with a hunger strike without a declared purpose. It's as though you were protesting somewhat along these lines: "I left a loving family, which certainly never encouraged me to be autonomous. I married Santo, hoping he would support me and together we would set up a good husband/wife rapport. I thought we could become a couple who would cross the street and visit my family together as husband and wife. However, I've become only an appendage who follows my husband and children when they visit my family. I didn't intend to break up with my folks, but I definitely thought we would have an independent married life. Santo is a perfect mother's pet and has burrowed in over there as though he were their son." Mrs. Bar, I bet you feel Santo gets along better with your folks than you do. Did he become their son more than you are their daughter?

Mrs. Bar: No, I don't think so!

Dr. Prata: Do you believe Santo's relationship with your parents is a filial one?

Mrs. Bar: Oh, definitely. Their relationship to Santo and his relationship with them is more than just a parent/offspring relationship.

Dr. Prata: List the offspring in order of importance. Who comes first?

Mrs. Bar: You mean, in my family?

Dr. Prata: Yes! Would you come first?

Mrs. Bar: Oh, no!

Dr. Prata: Lella, then? or Santo?

Mrs. Bar: Maybe, Santo. Yes, it would be Santo, I guess.

Dr. Prata: So that's why Lella has been trying to drag Roberto into the proceedings. She feels she's losing ground and Santo is getting ahead of her!

Lella: There's some truth in that.

Dr. Prata: This business of "two years" that keeps cropping up. *For two years* Lella has been saying: "Unless I can find a boyfriend my parents approve of and get him involved in the family, Santo will make off with everything! Everything as far as affection is concerned, and from a relational point of view. Every day he gets more important. If I bring in Roberto, that should give me some clout." Right?

Mrs. Bar: I don't know if things are exactly like that.

Dr. Prata: This happened two years ago, didn't it? Lella brought Roberto into the family. Lella felt threatened that Santo was getting too important.

Lella: As I see it, Santo was always very welcome, liked and loved by everyone. He didn't need to be charming and nice. He was accepted just like that.

Dr. Prata: Maria and Giuliana were also welcome. Mrs. Bar was hoping Giuliana would add some weight to her.

But all the girls have done is to enhance Santo's prestige. Lella, since you've not lost the most, you don't feel this so strongly. Your sister admits this, doesn't she? The loss of prestige is a serious thing, we come across it so often—I don't even have to look for it, it simply turns up in many families. In many cases there is some sort of shattered hope or a number of adverse circumstances.

In your case, Mrs. Bar, there wasn't enough time for you and Santo to build up your relationship as a couple. You didn't have the time to "break in" as a couple. When there's a baby on the way, there's an immediate and automatic tendency to start thinking as parents rather than as husband and wife. Isn't that right? No time for a "break in." Then Santo forsakes his own folks and digs in with your family. As I see it, he's become steadily more important and continues to become increasingly important to your family. Is that so, Mrs. Bar? (*Silence*)

I believe, during her second pregnancy, Erica began to think: "I'll give up hoping this child will help redefine the situation—I won't be able to be his real mother. When this child is born, Santo will get even more fatherly and motherly. He'll take the baby with him to my parents, and I'll become even more left out. Either I go with them and act as a dutiful daughter or, if I want to stay away, I lose altogether and won't mean anything anymore to this family— neither a daughter, a wife, nor a mother." Is that right?

Mrs. Bar:	Yes.
Dr. Prata:	Santo—may I call you Santo?
Mr. Bar:	Please do.
Dr. Prata:	Do you agree?
Mr. Bar:	I really don't know if my position has become better as time went by. I felt I had been accepted by this

family, a long while ago, before any of this started. Anyway, it's for the others to say.

Dr. Prata: You got to the top of the heap when Giuliana was born, is that true?

Mr. Bar: No, I thought I'd reached the top when I got married.

Dr. Prata: Surely your stock went on increasing after that.

Mr. Bar: It may have a bit when Maria was born, but it's been the same after that.

Dr. Prata: At any rate, it hasn't diminished. If anything, your value has increased, hasn't it?

Mr. Bar: Lately, I've been trying, consciously or unconsciously, to depreciate it because I, too, have come to realize that this state of affairs which suited me well *is* a bit unhealthy when seen from another point of view. I no longer am quite as content and as smug as before. If I was a misanthrope, I've grown to be more so now. So, I realize that something's bothering me. Something that has nothing to do with the idea of breaking loose from a comfortable situation.

Dr. Prata: Breaking loose isn't the point at all! I definitely don't want you to think that I'm suggesting that you detach yourself from the grandparents.

Mr. Bar: Oh, no. No.

Dr. Prata: What I'm saying is that you have, in this matter, assumed a very filial position in Mrs. Bar's family. You started taking Maria over there with you. You began working on the bonsai plants and now you've taken Giuliana along as well. Everyone goes trekking to the other side of the street except Erica. She has lost her identity as a person, as a wife, and as a mother.

Mr. Bar: Yes.

Dr. Prata: Your wife has gradually assumed the role of a daughter, which obliges her to heed everyone's advice.

What's lacking is a proper husband/wife rapport, as well as that of a mother and father.

Mr. Bar: Yes, but there has not been any escalation. I think I reached the maximum esteem, consent, consideration, and affection before the girls were born.

Dr. Prata: Quite so. However, in January or February, when Erica said: "There's another baby coming. At this point my position should improve . . ."

Mr. Bar: Yes?

Dr. Prata: ". . . and yet it's clearer than ever that I'm *not* Santo's wife, and I'm *not* the mother of these two little girls. The girls have caught on to this because—they don't come to me and ask: 'Mom, can I do this or that'; they go straight to their grandmother instead. They've figured out this lopsided hierarchy perfectly. They know that their grandparents rank highest—they're really the parents, and then comes Santo . . ."

Mr. Bar: Right.

Dr. Prata: ". . . who acts like an elder brother, and then comes Lella, in her normal role of a daughter, and then come three little sisters, Erica, Maria, and Giuliana, three little grandchildren and they are all on an equal footing. . . ."

Mr. Bar: Because of this hunger strike, lots of things have come to light lately. I spoke to the psychologist at the hospital about it. I have this paternalistic manner towards my wife. It's quite true that there isn't a proper husband/wife rapport between us. It's also true that my paternalistic attitude intensified when I discovered I had to take on the role of a custodial father as well. Especially since Erica started to increase this anorexic behavior. . . .

Dr. Prata: This strike maneuver was designed to counter the position in which a subverted hierarchy had placed her.

Mr. Bar:	Yes, I found myself acting as a father to yet another little daughter, to prevent her from getting into trouble.
Dr. Prata:	So, here is your wife, who leaves a custodial family to marry you, hoping that you will help her set up first a proper relationship as a couple and then a family that won't be an appendage tagged on to her former family. Instead, she finds herself saddled with a husband who becomes a son to her family and acts like a father towards her—and a watchdog father, at that.
Mr. Bar:	Yes, a second father.
Dr. Prata:	Don't you agree that Erica seems to have had more than her share of surveillance?
Mr. Bar:	Well, yes, but all the surveillance began when my wife's behavior started to deteriorate . . .
Dr. Prata:	The way I see it, Erica didn't have a clear idea in her mind at the start. However, something made her lose hope and say: "This second child of mine isn't going to change a thing." This, in fact, was something Erica began telling herself before she even discovered that she was pregnant again.
Mr. Bar:	I think so, yes.
Dr. Prata:	So she started this hunger strike. All this may not have been clear enough for her to actually express it, so she resorted to the strike maneuver, without providing any explanation.
Mr. Bar:	This paternalistic attitude may date even further back than the past six years; it may already have been there when we got married. During the first four years . . .
Dr. Prata:	Look, Santo, you were the one who went across the street, right? You became like a son to them. Mind you, all this is quite fine and it's certainly not something that should be changed, God forbid. It's just

	that the relationships have grown to be hopelessly lopsided.
Mr. Bar:	Well, I fail to see how one can call it an abnormal rapport. It doesn't affect me in such a way as to . . .
Dr. Prata:	There's this very deep affection, and all the bonsai plants are there to prove it. No one could consider this wrong or harmful in any way. However, when a boat careens so heavily to one side, one starts thinking that something must be done to get it on an even keel again. If not, the sailing may be rough. What was missing, above all, was a proper husband/wife relationship, and beyond that an upgrading of Erica's status as a mother, particularly as the mother of these two little girls.
Mr. Bar:	Yes.
Dr. Prata:	Mr. Marco, I'm sure you'll agree that hierarchy is a very important factor. I don't know how many people are working for you, but if an assistant gardener were to come along and start giving you advice . . .
Grandfather:	I see!
Dr. Prata:	You'd put him in his place immediately, wouldn't you? We have an upset hierarchy, whereby your daughter has become a little sister to her own little daughters! It's as though she weren't properly qualified to . . .
Grandfather:	There's another thing that's important. Santo's a doctor and works in a hospital. He leaves home early in the morning and gets back late. When he's on night duty, he'll come home, eat, and rush back to the hospital to spend the night there. It's not just that we're so very fond of him. It's this full-time job as a doctor that has ruined their family life.
Dr. Prata:	You mean, it's made them depend on you a lot more?
Grandfather:	No, not that. You see, we know what type of man Santo is, and what kind of family he comes from. His work at the hospital means everything to him.

It's what comes first. He does his work very, very thoroughly.

Dr. Prata: I see, and he comes home and then spends a lot of time with his children, before going over to the garden to work on the bonsais. So Erica is fourth in line?

Grandfather: Yes, often there just isn't enough time.

Dr. Prata: So, there's no harm meant. It's just that they haven't had time for a proper run-through as a couple and this is something that makes itself felt. This imbalance, with Santo being more of a son to you than a husband to Erica. Santo is definitely the little girls' father, but Erica isn't their mother. More so since the girls can go to their Grandma and if their Grandma says: "It's all right," that's all they need. It's as if there were these three little sisters, all on equal footing, but this makes for a considerable muddle. . . .

Mr. Bar: Well, all I can say is, I'm not the one who goes fussing over the girls, they're the ones who fuss over me; they're always climbing in my lap, you see? I'm not your typical father. . . .

Dr. Prata: You don't have to be; your rank in this family is far superior to your wife's. . . .

Mr. Bar: I have charisma.

Dr. Prata: Let's say you hold a higher rank, your stock is rated higher, if we want to speak in market terminology. So, the girls always come to you, and this raises the value of your stock even higher. All Erica can do is take the elevator to the cellar. It's Erica's job to care for the children, and do all the tiresome things for them. Things the children resent and get on their nerves.

Mr. Bar: Right.

Dr. Prata: Whereas all the prestige, affectionate things, have shifted over to Dad and the grandparents.

Mr. Bar: Yes, we're quite aware of this, because Erica often says: "Look at the girls, they always run to you, and I'm left having to do all the necessary, bothersome, unpleasant day-to-day things. Whenever they want anything, they come running to you. . . ." I usually answer: "That may be so, but it depends on your attitude, you know, your attitude is different."

Dr. Prata: Well, of course it's an attitude one might expect from someone who ends up constantly in the cellar even when she keeps pushing the "up" button in the elevator.

Mr. Bar: Right, the attitude of someone who's even given up trying.

Dr. Prata: Erica did make an effort. She tried to have another child, but when she saw that even this second child would not be of any use, she said to herself: "At this point I'll go on a hunger strike and hope they'll finally sit up and take notice." This boomeranged and caused her stock to slump even more severely.

Mr. Bar: Right.

Dr. Prata: Poor thing, it's like she's a little girl and one has to watch and see if she eats or doesn't eat, whether she sits on her potty every day, and so forth . . . all this has brought her steadily further down towards a child's level.

Mr. Bar Yes, it's backfired on her.

Dr. Prata: Yes, it surely has. Still, there may be something the others can do about this because she can't manage to boost the value of her stock all by herself.

Mr. Bar: I guess so.

Dr. Prata: I'll go and discuss this with my team now. (*Dr. Prata goes out, and returns.*)

We always have to decide what should be done, and whether family therapy is appropriate. In your case, we would like to meet again, look into things more closely. This doesn't mean there will be 11 sessions in all; there'll only be 10, as I told you before. I wish to thank Lella and the grandparents for coming today; they don't need to come next time. We'll only be seeing the four of you.

Mr. Bar: The girls, too?

Dr. Prata: Yes, the four of you. Your appointment is for Tuesday, October 21, at 2:15 P.M.

They begin to leave and say goodbye. The grandparents thank me for asking them to come. Then:

Grandmother: Maria, Giuliana, come along!

Maria: No, we'll go down with Mom.

They get into the elevator in turns, first the grandparents and Lella, then the parents with their two little girls. Such instant feedback is highly significant. It shows that the children have grasped the fact that their mother's problem also depends on their treating her like a sister, on their relying on their grandparents too heavily.

The second session, with the nuclear family, validated my "Withdrawal of Significant Ones" hypothesis. Mrs. Bar confirmed it, saying that, at a certain point, she felt "like a deserted woman watching, from the window of a winter palace, her husband, children, and parents talking and enjoying themselves in a summer house surrounded by azaleas, roses, and bonsais."

We decided family therapy was needed. The parents were invited to the third session, but not the two girls. In this case we also used the New Method. Mr. and Mrs. Bar followed the prescriptions with great diligence . . . and without any change whatsoever. From the very first session, I investigated if the fact that Mr. Bar was a doctor and had suggested my center was a problem. Mrs. Bar swore it wasn't. Certainly, she would have phoned because she really wanted to solve her problems. A specialist in the field of anorexia was exactly what she desperately needed from the beginning. But the display of her skeletonlike frame in the hospital and town where Santo worked and lived was a vendetta Mrs. Bar would not renounce.

She had already "destroyed" all the physicians Santo had suggested. Now my turn had come.

During the eighth session, it became clear that Mrs. Bar would never give up her hunger strike while I was in charge of a treatment suggested by her husband. We discontinued family therapy.

Follow-up

Eight months later, on May 30, 1988, I phoned and spoke with Mr. and Mrs. Bar. We allowed more time than usual before doing this follow-up because, in our opinion, such a heavy game needed a longer interval for our input to work.

Mr. Bar seemed happy to receive my telephone call. He was cordial and thankful. Therapy, he said, had had a positive effect on him. He seemed to me less condescending and more "simpático" than usual. He had stopped interfering with Erica's food, weight, and behavioral problems. Although he was not in love, he had started dating a nurse and had not informed Erica. His career was going very well; he was now the head of a department.

A husband's unfaithfulness to his wife is usually not considered good behavior. But for Santo, who in the "symmetrical game" with his wife had always played the Golden Man, the Golden Husband and Father, the long suffering Martyr, to be unfaithful means that he has given up being so perfect and without reproach. He seems to have moved into a more human role—the role of a husband who is fed up waiting for his wife to give up her hunger strike. For the moment he informs only his colleagues and the therapist of his "change," his "imperfect behavior," but this unfaithfulness seems to be a valuable starting point for this "saint" who wants to become a human being. Within the context of this family, Santo's dating a nurse and not informing his wife could be considered a good outcome.

Maria and Giuliana were also doing well. Thanks to the *disappearances*, they were more autonomous and self-sufficient. For example, they were now going to school alone. Grandfather Marco, after his wife died of cancer, sold his land and retired. Lella lives with him and Roberto spends his free time with them. "It is clear to me that he is doing exactly what I did before," said Mr. Bar.

Dr. Prata:	How is Erica?
Mr. Bar:	She didn't change much after the therapy. She weighs 99 pounds and is still amenorrheic. After the last session, I gave up making suggestions and doing therapeutic interventions.
Dr. Prata:	I was afraid that you would take Erica to another therapist and fail again.
Mr. Bar:	No, I perfectly understoood you when you said that no matter what treatment or therapist I suggested, Erica would sabotage the effort. Consequently, I did nothing at all! Erica didn't look for anyone else.
Dr. Prata:	Maybe she's waiting for you to fall into a trap, Mr. Bar.
Mr. Bar:	Maybe!

He said their relationship had changed. It is not an easy one, but they had never spoken of a separation. Mr. Bar spends less time with the children, while Erica enjoys playing and spending more time than before with them. Sometimes he is fed up with his wife because they have a poor sexual life. Erica is more friendly, but still difficult to understand. At this point, I asked him if I could speak with Mrs. Bar. He agreed and, after thanking me for the therapy, called Mrs. Bar to the phone.

Erica was cordial and "simpática." In fact, she was more relaxed than before. She said she had continued the hunger strike and was still thin. She was torn between saying stop and let's go on. She had discontinued taking laxatives and diuretics, and was only dieting. Twice, she had even stuffed herself a bit without running to the toilet to force vomit. Her relationship with their children was much better. They had become more obedient and affectionate. She confirmed that after the "*disappearances*" the children had become more autonomous.

Mrs. Bar:	Should we "disappear" again?
Dr. Prata:	It is up to you. You threw me out because I had been chosen by your husband. You would sabotage every-

thing I said to demonstrate that I was wrong and
Santo had made a mistake in choosing me. (*We both
burst out laughing.*) At what point are you with your
vendetta? I don't know what I would do if I were you.
Surely, Santo is becoming more handsome every
day, while Maria and Giuliana are growing up. Very
soon, actually sooner than you expect, they will become more involved with their own lives and pay
more attention to themselves and their friends than
to their parents.

Contrarily, Erica, you have become uglier and uglier every day. Just look at yourself in a mirror and
compare it to an old picture of yourself and see the
difference. Your hair, skin, and bones are wasting
away. See if the game has been worthwhile, or is it
just a Pyrrhic victory? "Another victory like this and
we will be ruined." Your mother died. Your father
retired, but nothing has changed. I said you are a
therapist headhunter. My head is not very beautiful,
but maybe if you hang it on a gold chain around your
neck, it will show up as a trophy. (*Laughing.*) My
best wishes to you.

Mrs. Bar: Thank you, Giuliana. I believe I will soon call you.
When I do, you will immediately know I've decided
to give up my strike and want to change.

Comment

Although they had been left alone and the therapist had openly
withdrawn from the field, admitting defeat, eight months had not
been enough to change the game. It had only become less rigid and
a little more bearable. We were under the impression that Mr. and
Mrs. Bar were no longer unhappy together, but that they were
watching each other just like two boxers who, after having given
each other deadly punches, start fearing the opponent but still
haven't decided whether they would resume the fight or find a
decent way to leave the ring.

Nevertheless, there were a few elements which allowed us to

hope for a positive development: (1) The two daughters were less involved in the family game than before. They no longer were totally on their father's side and seemed to have an affectionate and peaceful relationship with both the father and mother. (2) Mr. Bar had stopped interfering in his wife's decisions and had resisted the temptation to urge her to make one more unsuccessful therapeutic attempt. Moreover, the perfect and irreproachable Mr. Bar was becoming a little less "Santo," a little less of an angel, and a little more of a man since he was looking elsewhere for the sexual satisfaction Erica had been granting him only halfheartedly for years. (3) Mrs. Bar wasn't the acid person we had met any longer. She had learned how to laugh at herself. She was openly calling her refusing food a "hunger strike" and she was confessing that the decision to go on with it or not depended only on her.

We have had other cases in which we have tested the "Withdrawal of Significant Ones" hypothesis, for instance, that of the Proti family, which we will present in Chapter 4, when referring to the Second Session.

3
The Working Method

Since Dr. Selvini and I introduced the New Method in family therapy, 10 years have passed and it has been tested not only with psychotics and schizophrenics but also with anorexics and other seriously disturbed families. In my opinion, the New Method represents, for the time being, the most effective approach towards a better understanding and resolution of family "games" (Selvini Palazzoli, 1986).

Social changes and fashion will always supply new roles and new "games," but therapists must always endeavor to be current and effective in working out new interventions. For example, hard drugs and AIDS, the scourges of the last part of this century, have introduced heavy, damaging "games" which have required intervention. The New Method seems to work with drug addicts, but my statistics are too limited to be probatory. It would be interesting to test this technique on a large number of drug addicts. In this case it would become mandatory to work in connection with hospitals equipped to deal with those aspects lying outside the family therapy context and control.

When the New Method proved more effective than the paradoxes, Dr. Selvini and I abandoned paradoxical therapy and shifted to a prescriptive one. Our explanation of its greater effectiveness was that a family can easily disconnect itself and cut off verbal messages but it cannot disconnect itself when engaged in an action: it acts or it refuses to act. Both "actions" will be for the therapist a piece of information which will be more difficult to disguise than a word. As I have said (Selvini Palazzoli & Prata,

1982a), "The question is on what hypothesis is this new method based? Giving the schizophrenic families a fixed, invariable prescription structures for the therapists a repeatable context. A repeatable context supplies the optimal condition for learning about 'schizophrenia' " (pp. 239–240).

Until now, I have been unable to introduce into my repertory another technique as effective as the New Method. It evolved from the experience that making a family act was more effective than making a family talk. It was mainly based on the hypothesis that the "identified patient feels somehow cheated" and wants to get his revenge. I can say that with the New Method I have seen many cheating "games" stopped, with the I.P. leaving the field and being "cured." The more I test this technique, the more I trust it and know the difficulties involved in its practical application.

There are particular cases where the New Method doesn't work. For example, I tried several times to use it with families who had adopted children, but when I come to the question of the *evening disappearances* the parents usually refuse to follow the prescription. They want to help their children, but they don't feel capable of leaving them alone. Even after many years of adoption, adoptive parents seem to have a sense of responsibility that is different from that of natural parents. A technique taking into account the difficulties of adoptive parents is discussed in Chapter 9.

Nor does the New Method work with families having psychopathic patients because, in those families, not only the children but also the parents refuse to obey rules. During the session, each member of the family will do his or her best to disrupt the conversation, behaving in a very insubordinate, challenging, and even provocative way towards the therapist. Even when the parents declare themselves ready to undergo family therapy, they will disregard the prescription, change the sentences, come without the *notes*, break *the secret*, and transform everything into a terrible mess.

We know that psychopathic families can also disregard legal rules or obey them merely out of fear. Maybe a technique based on some easier prescriptions and shorter intervals than the New Method could work more satisfactorily with them, but I have not enough experience to suggest anything specific.

In 1979, when Dr. Selvini and I developed the New Method, we started without expecting it to become a very creative phase of our research. Every day we had new situations to face and new questions to answer—and these still arise today. The interesting discoveries are not over, but I can understand the reluctance of therapists to use this technique. It seems to be awfully repetitive and boring. However, it is just the opposite. In any event, one accepts even the boring solfeggio when one is really motivated to play the piano. Then, the more one practices, the more one masters the instrument and enjoys playing it. Later I will discuss this technique in detail.

Telephone calls always come to my center from families with seriously disturbed members. At the beginning, Dr. Selvini and I were using the New Method more or less indiscriminately with the majority of the most disturbed families, taking for granted that they were willing to do everything to put an end to their discomfort. We were wrong. Some unexpected failures proved that not all families were prepared to face the difficulties and risks connected with the rules and different stages of this technique. We discovered that even when family therapy was needed, before making a decision it was necessary to explore the motivations and the expectations of each family member.

Within certain limits, what a therapist needs are *parents* motivated for family therapy and willing to work with him. The relational aspect is also of the greatest importance. A therapist has to take into account the relationship he has established with the family members. For instance, when the contact with the children, whether it is positive or negative, is intriguing and captivating, all the following steps of the therapy—*excluding them from the sessions, declaring the secret, disappearing from home,* and so on—will have a stronger effect.

Another objective a systemic therapist tries to reach while working with the family is to shift the spotlight from the I.P. to the disturbed interaction within the family. Obviously, he is not interested in the trivial jealousies between the siblings that all families are riddled with and so willing to present to him on a golden platter. Those are merely exhibited and linear causes meant to camouflage the hidden conflicts which maintain the family "game" and rules. A therapist's interest is to see how convinced all the members of the family are, after two sessions, that the family's problems do not come only from the disturbed behavior of the I.P., but also from conflicts and misunderstandings within the family.

The New Method can also be used when the I.P. is a member of a couple, or one of the parents, or even a single parent. It will be more difficult to motivate the family and surmount some practical difficulties, but it works. If it doesn't work, it is not due to the technique, but rather to our mistakes in conducting the therapy or to the reluctance of a family (which hasn't plumbed the depths yet).

In any event, I still feel excited about confronting and solving new difficulties with each family. The personal pleasure of deciphering family "games," which are not infinite, only adds to the therapeutic pleasure of discovering, and breaking imbroglios and freeing the family from the "games" it has become entangled in. There is also the intellectual pleasure of finding new facets of this prescription, knowing that it has still "en réserve" unexplored levels.

THE FIRST SESSION

In the therapy room we place one chair for each member of the family, plus one or two "free chairs" and another one for the therapist. I suggest avoiding sofas. When the family arrives, it is not the therapist but a supervisor who welcomes them and leaves them alone in the therapy room. The team can observe from behind the mirror their spontaneous seating arrangement. The way the "free chair" is used is sometimes amazing. For example, in winter a mother could refuse to leave her coat in the dressing room, advancing fully dressed, with hat, coat, and umbrella, convoying the family into the therapy room. There she puts her bag on a chair, takes everyone's heavy clothing, piles it onto a "free chair," and sits down in a strategic position. She could give the chair she has "reserved" with her bag to "someone," leaving "someone" else behind the wall. Hundreds of analogic orders are given in a few minutes. The "spontaneous seating arrangement" is never accidental and it is extremely informative.

To put into the therapy room small chairs and toys for the children is nonsense. Small chairs are an implicit order given to the children where the therapist wants them to sit. The spontaneous seating arrangement would be completely disrupted and, consequently, give no information at all. My colleagues keep telling me that they give small chairs and toys to the children "because they care for them." In my opinion, it's a sign of compliance and contempt. As a child, I wouldn't appreciate being invited with all my family to a family session, which sounds so important, and be given a small chair and toys! I could take with me my Teddy Bear and sit on the floor, but I would be offended at being treated as a small baby. I never give small chairs and toys.

Very seldom do children come with a toy. If they ask for it or for food, it is informative to see whom they address and for what. Usually, they sit on a chair, listen, and participate. Hours of television have given them the ability to sit for lengthy periods without causing any disturbance. Besides, I don't want to create any confusion. *I'm not there to take care of the children. I'm there to lead a therapeutic session,* to catch information, formulate hypotheses on their "game," and solve painful situations. I avoid giving the least instruction or indication which could distort information.

Young couples with small children are liable to be still very closely attached to their respective families of origin, particularly to their parents. When the I.P. is a child, a member of the third generation, we must remember, when formulating hypotheses, that a member of the first generation may be playing an important part in the "game." Thus, in filling out the chart, we must try to find out who that person is and include him/her in the first session. Then, if during the session there is a child—usually the I.P.—who disturbs to the point of making verbal exchange impossible, we can hypothesize that the I.P. is behaving like a soldier obeying an expressed or implicit order given by his general. If one succeeds in unmasking this general, the maneuver can be thwarted and his identity bared. After this is done, all the noisiness ceases and the session can proceed.

Often, the general is a grandmother or an aunt. For instance, we might say: "Our experience tells us that when a child so disturbs a session he does it because someone who is important to him is against family therapy and has come to this session unwillingly." Then, if there is a sibling of the I.P., we ask him to make a list starting from the most willing to come to the one least willing. The list should include all those present at the session. When this investigation is over, we can ask how important members of the family who were not invited had expressed themselves towards this therapy.

When a family comes without a member of the nuclear family whose presence had been clearly requested, the therapist enters the room and asks why that person hasn't come and dismisses the family without doing the session and without making them pay. If the absent one doesn't belong to the nuclear family, the team decides case by case if the session can be carried out or not (Prata, 1987).

I always explain how we work while making the telephone chart. Entering the therapy room, the therapist begins the session by giving the same information about the camera, the mirror, and the team behind it: "My cotherapists are there to help me and will probably call me out during the session to make suggestions." I don't introduce the team, but I do nothing to conceal them. For example, a member of the team, welcoming the family, will introduce himself. Then, if someone wants to look behind the mirror, he can do so when the therapist goes for a discussion with the team in another room. This member of the family will meet the camera operator, who will be available for explanations. Everything is done openly, and, generally, the family does not react negatively to the equipment or to the team behind the mirror. They already know that the therapist and the supervisors are professionals unitedly working for them.

If the therapist loses the thread or misses a hint, the supervisor will knock on the door. The therapist will exit and on returning he will look rescued. One may surprise the family by investigating in a completely new direction, picking up a "hint" he had previously disregarded. Making a connection between two events which didn't seem important, he may even arrive at an important discovery and uncover the "game." Young children actively participate in the session when they become involved.

In *Paradox and Counterparadox* (Selvini Palazzoli et al., 1978a) and in *Hypothesizing—Circularity—Neutrality* (Selvini Palazzoil et al., 1980b) we explained our way of conducting the session, as did Dr. Viaro (Viaro & Leonardi, 1982), our associate. Dr. Raffin

(1988) has made an epistemological comment on the session, which I am going to explain. I will start with the beginning of a first session to demonstrate how we put into practice theories and techniques (Popper, 1963).

The Sele Family

The Seles (see page 28) were an intelligent and educated family of six from Ravenna. They collaborated actively and the infrequent insubordinations were mainly committed by Mr. Sele and the identified patient.

I had to test two hypotheses: (1) Was Gino, the firstborn, the only son, a physician, and the one who called me, *that prestigious sibling?* (2) Was Ida, Mrs. Sele's sister, "instigating" the I.P. against Mr. Sele, with Mrs. Sele as an accomplice?

By the end of the second session, I was able to discard the first hypothesis. The second hypothesis, which surfaced during the first session, proved true in the second and third sessions.

First Session—October 8, 1985

Invited to the session: The parents, the four children, and Ida, Mrs. Sele's sister.

The beginning of the session is a typical example of how we start working with the family in the first session. But I want to underline a difference. Usually, when a person who has been invited doesn't come to the session, we immediately inquire about his/her absence. In this case, since the "absent" was our "second hypothesis," I decided to postpone the investigation concerning Mrs. Sele's sister.

Spontaneous seating arrangement:

Mrs. Sele °	° Carla	° Maria
Mr. Sele °		° Bianca
		° Gino

° Dr. Prata
_____

Mirror

Dr. Prata:	There should have been . . .
Mrs. Sele:	I hoped my sister Ida would come, but she caught the flu and . . .
Dr. Prata:	Anyway, she's not here. I explained on the phone the way we work. We're a team; my supervisors are behind the one-way mirror. They may call me out if they have something to tell me. I've already talked with Gino. Now I'd like to hear how the parents see the problem. (*to Mrs. Sele*) Would you tell me your point of view about the situation?
Mrs. Sele:	It's distressing. Maria had other episodes of great anxiety, but she's always bounced back.
Dr. Prata:	Can you recall how this started?
Mrs. Sele:	Yes. Five years ago . . . but recently it really got worse. Maria wanted to die, wanted to quit her studies. She was so anguished she couldn't understand anything. This lasted from February till October. After that she reemerged, thanks to psychotherapy, or medication, or maybe just on her own. One day she would say: "That's enough, I'm going back to studying." After the third episode, though, this phase lasted for a long time. From October until last July, she worked hard on her dissertation. In November, she graduated with honors. During the winter, it all started again and she lost weight.
Dr. Prata:	Was this a problem?
Mrs. Sele:	No, because Maria likes to be slim, she doesn't like the way she is now. This coincided with one of her stand-in teaching jobs, temporary jobs they were, lasting a week.
Dr. Prata:	Did she become anxious during the last of these short-term jobs?
Mrs. Sele:	Yes, last February. She hadn't mastered the subject she was expected to teach. She also had some personal problems and this time Maria is having more trouble getting out of it.

Dr. Prata: No, just tell me your conclusion. You say it started five years ago. What do you think may have caused these problems?

Mrs. Sele: Maria had some unhappy love affairs. This may bring one loneliness and distress.

Dr. Prata: You mean, there were boyfriends? (*To Mr. Sele*) Do you agree with your wife?

Mr. Sele: Yes. I'd like to add something: Maria is a girl who takes everything very seriously. She's that way about her studies, too. She magnifies things. It was like that when she was at university. When she didn't know a subject perfectly, she would remain home. Preparing exams, she went through such anguish . . .

Dr. Prata: You mean, there was this excessive worrying about grades. Mrs Sele said it may have something to do with boyfriends. Did the family reject someone she cared for? How was the family's attitude towards her boyfriends? What about her friends, were they usually welcomed by the family, or weren't they?

Maria: There's always a lot of interfering.

Dr. Prata: Who does the interfering, mostly?

Maria: (*Several voices speak at once*) Our parents interfere in different things; they both do.

Dr. Prata: You mean, they disapprove of your friends? Were your friends, boys and girls, welcomed or not?

Maria: My girlfriends were welcomed.

Dr. Prata: What about classmates, were they welcomed?

Maria: Yes.

Dr. Prata: For example, when you started having a fancy for a boy, did they object? (*Long pause*)

Maria: They started objecting after the neurologist said I should avoid . . .

Dr. Prata: Falling in love?

Maria:	. . . because my emotional sphere is peculiar . . . (*she weeps*).
Dr. Prata:	It had already started, hadn't it? I mean, whenever you liked a boy, he wouldn't be . . .
Maria:	Yes, even before this, no one was acceptable, for one reason or another.
Dr. Prata:	Did they speak to the boy, telling him you had a "peculiar emotional sphere"? Or did your parents speak to you directly?
Maria:	They'd say he wasn't the right type for me.
Dr. Prata:	Was he really the wrong type, or was there that "emotional sphere"?
Maria:	The neurologist hadn't come into the picture yet.
Dr. Prata:	Were things the same with Gino? (*To Gino*) Were your friends mostly disapproved of? You told me you married Alma against your parents' wishes. Before that, you were living with her and they had already disapproved.
Gino:	I was a leftist during high school, I am still a leftist. My friends weren't welcomed, but I wasn't forbidden to go out with them. I was free to see who I pleased. When my story with Alma began, there was fierce opposition at home.
Dr. Prata:	Why?
Gino:	For a lot of reasons.
Dr. Prata:	(*To Mr. Sele*) Can you tell me why you opposed this affair?
Mr. Sele:	I'm from the South. I've had a very strict upbringing, I just couldn't see my son and Alma living together—mixing with my family socially. Besides, I was worried about his three sisters.
Dr. Prata:	Worried about the bad example, you mean?
Mr. Sele:	Exactly. I did a lot of arguing with that girl, and she said: "How could I harm Bianca?" Bianca was seven at the time. "What does it matter to Bianca if Gino

and I live together? It's quite common." I said: "Do what you want in your house, not here!"

Dr. Prata: You mean they were going to bed in your home?

Mr. Sele: No, no, no! It's just a way of speaking (*the girls laugh*), just the arguments we'd have at home. I was brought up that way, I've tried to raise my children and my family along the same lines. I succeeded in part, but I failed for the most part.

Dr. Prata: The one who gave you the most trouble has been Gino?

Mr. Sele: Yes.

Dr. Prata: Even as a child?

Mr. Sele: Oh no, no, no! All of them were good students, highly regarded by their teachers. We were proud of them in every way! I've always been so proud of them until the time the girls were 17 or 18.

Dr. Prata: Were you prouder of Gino then of Maria? There's only a year's difference between them. (*To Maria*) In your opinion, was he prouder of Gino because he was a boy? Or for other reasons?

Maria: Because he was a boy and because he did better in school. Our family has always been a very happy and peaceful one. Quite enviably so!

Dr. Prata: All of you toed the line?

Maria: Yes.

Dr. Prata: What about your mother? Did she share your father's views on how you ought to be brought up?

Maria: No. Anyway the key to everything . . .

Dr. Prata: (*To Mrs. Sele*) Where are you from?

Mrs. Sele: I'm a Catholic, I'm not from Ravenna.

Maria: (*Interrupting and raising her voice*) If we got good grades, we were allowed to do sports and meet with our friends. Although no one ever said it, this was the . . .

Dr. Prata:	They used it as a touchstone. You said Gino did better than you. Was he very much better? How good was he?
Maria:	Yes, he was.
Mrs. Sele:	(*Butting in*) Without half trying, too!
Dr. Prata:	I notice Carla doesn't agree. . . . (*To Carla*) How were things?
Carla:	We never had problems in high school. There would be the occasional low grade in Latin, but school work wasn't ever an issue. I'm the only one who repeated a subject.
Dr. Prata:	Was it a tragedy?
Carla:	Absolutely not. If Maria says there was this black-mail, that is, "as long as you do well, do whatever you want . . ."
Dr. Prata:	Since you made them proud anyway . . .
Carla:	Yes, other things may have had a part in it, but our school record wasn't so important.
Dr. Prata:	So, you have a different point of view. You say: "Gino was more highly regarded . . ."
Maria:	The difference between Gino and me is that he had such a good memory (*noise and laughter in the background*), whereas I always had problems memorizing.
Dr. Prata:	You needed to do more cramming. He got by with less effort, and has this gift of the gab, so he could put himself across more easily. . . .
Mrs. Sele:	Besides, he was less tense and nervous.
Maria:	He succeeded in sports, too.
Mr. Sele:	(*Butting in*) Doctor, may I . . .
Dr. Prata:	No. I will listen to you in a minute. Was there this higher regard for Gino when you were children?
Maria:	That's the way I felt. When he started becoming the bad guy, I became the good one, good at school, affectionate, ready to help out at home.

Dr. Prata:	When did he start becoming the bad guy?
Maria:	When he left home. He was considered a rebel.
Dr. Prata:	Carla, was he a wicked or a rebellious son? Rebellion carries all sorts of positive overtones. Was he considered the reprobate who had lost his parents' esteem and respect, or someone who managed to do a lot of glamorous and exciting things?
Carla:	With three girls and one firstborn son, there's always this tendency to see Gino in a special light. He's the only boy. The rebel role he played in the family was important because he was the only one who could stand up to Dad. I was 14 then, Gino's was the only personality strong enough to try to make a stand against Dad.
Dr. Prata:	Which of you three girls would you say admired Gino the most?
Carla:	The three of us!
Dr. Prata:	Oh, all three of you worshipped him!
Maria:	I felt this so strongly that I had to do some redimensioning of it during my analysis.
Dr. Prata:	Redimensioning in what way?
Maria:	(*Long silence*)
Dr. Prata:	He was good at school. He had a good memory, and could express himself well. What else? Before he lived with Alma, what did Gino do to be considered a rebel? He had quite an audience, with three sisters worshipping him. So, I'd think maybe he would do all this to show off.
Mr. Sele:	He never was a rebel! His teacher got him involved in politics during his second year of high school. His revolt started when he switched from the strict and confining atmosphere of Ravenna. Even though before that there was plenty of leeway for him, trips abroad, etc. His real rebellion started when he achieved absolute freedom and moved away from his family during his first university year in Bologna.

Dr. Prata:	Which year?
Gino:	The second year, 1973–1974.
Dr. Prata:	So during his second year in Bologna?
Mr. Sele:	The first year he passed all his exams. He rented a little apartment with a fellow student during his second year. Then he met that girl and began getting . . .
Dr. Prata:	(*To Maria*) There was more consideration for Gino only because of these two aspects. Actually, you never deserved less recognition, nor did he do anything to deserve more of it. Right? You also said: "I worshipped Gino and went on worshipping him for a long time." What made you worship him so? Why did you have this crush on him? Which parent had the strongest crush on Gino, Mom or Dad? (*Voices:* Dad did). What about you three sisters? Dad was the most infatuated with Gino.
Maria:	Yes, definitely.
Dr. Prata:	Who came next?
Maria:	(*long silence*) Me.
Dr. Prata:	You, Maria?
Mrs. Sele:	Yes, Maria (*laughs*).
Dr. Prata:	You mean, in your analysis it took all this digging to reappraise this?
Maria:	I guess so.
Dr. Prata:	Who comes next, in the ranking order?
Maria:	Either Carla or Bianca, I don't know. (*Voices of the sisters saying,* "Mom, Mom!" *Laughing*)
Mrs. Sele:	Not me!
Dr. Prata:	Who does Mom have a special crush on?
Maria:	On me.
Dr. Prata:	On you?
Maria:	Yes.

Dr. Prata: Always? Dad always singled out Gino as his favorite, that's settled . . .

Mr. Sele: I want to object.

Dr. Prata: Hold on a minute, please. (*To Maria*) You say, Mom always had a special weakness for you?

Maria: Yes, she always protected me the most.

Dr. Prata: Protection is something one can also give a poor creature.

Maria: Yes, but Mom valued me highly!

Dr. Prata: Was there more protection or more appreciation?

Maria: I have to say there was more appreciation until I said: "That's enough, I'm sick of all this studying." After that, there was a lot of protecting and encouragement to urge me on, and get me to reconsider. So much so that it aroused my sisters' jealousy.

Dr. Prata: Was your father protective towards you?

Maria: It was a different kind of protection. Mom's was more loving. Dad's was due to lack of esteem, I think.

Dr. Prata: So, Dad never held you in great esteem. Not even before you stopped studying? There was quite a gap, then, between Dad's esteem for Gino and what he had for you. Right from the start there was quite a big difference, wasn't there?

Maria: I guess so. I don't remember. I got praised if I did something useful in the house or got top grades. Otherwise . . .

Dr. Prata: Whereas Gino got all the approval without having to do anything for it? Mom's appreciation for you balanced things up a bit, by matching what Gino got from Dad? But Mom's esteem for you didn't really give you satisfaction.

Maria: It didn't make me feel all that good.

Dr. Prata: Let's hear from Carla. How did your parents balance out regarding their esteem for Bianca?

Carla:	It was right, I think.
Dr. Prata:	It's not a matter of right or wrong. We might have Dad preferring Bianca and Mom preferring Carla, or vice versa.
Carla:	No, their preferences were distributed more evenly, towards me and Bianca.
Dr. Prata:	The big difference only concerned the two firstborn.
Carla:	Yes, We call it "the birthright" (*laughs*). It's like a hot potato getting tossed from one child to the next. It went to Maria after the upheaval about Gino during his "roaring twenties." Six years ago it passed to me. As for Bianca, I don't know if she has already disappointed my father or my mother. Anyway, Bianca comes of age now and Mom and Dad seem to be passing this "birthright" to her.
Dr. Prata:	I see. What does it imply? This hot potato means more demands made on you? Less demands, . . . or what?
Mrs. Sele:	Expectations, rather.
Carla:	Fulfilled expectations! More responsibility! One isn't only responsible for oneself but for what one does, and also for the possible consequence to the other family members.
Dr. Prata:	"Now it's got down to me." Do you mean that Gino was the one most involved in these expectations, these responsibilities?
Carla:	I don't know how he felt about them. I believe he, too, went through them. First he was the "male child," the pivotal one, then the token was passed to Maria.
Maria:	I think Dad's life—more than Mom's . . . because Mom is more of an independent spirit—hinged on family and work. The first hard blow to hit Dad was the "disappointments" he received from Gino. This touched off . . . I don't know if it caused something to split inside of him, a bitterness, anyway. So here

was Dad who could make you feel full of anger and full of pity at once (*her voice breaks with emotion*). And here we were, feeling anger and pity for ourselves.

Dr. Prata: Did Dad's disappointment mainly concern Gino's political views? Or does it concern Alma?

Maria: Yes, Alma.

Dr. Prata: What happened when he married her?

Maria: He slowed down studying—trying to manage both things at once.

Dr. Prata: His marriage and his studies?

Gino: And my work, too.

Maria: And his work, which allowed him to be independent.

Dr. Prata: (*To Gino*) When you were living at home, whom did your parents turn to and confide in more?

Gino: During high school, I can't recall us ever being entrusted with anything, or being a confidant to Dad or Mom. Regarding the four of us, I was a bit closer to Maria. Actually, my memories of Maria are only that of playing together. In high school we separated. We had different interests. When I had a problem, I talked it over with my friends.

Dr. Prata: I didn't mean that. I meant who would your parents confide in?

Gino: Until I was 18, my parents would never take any of us into their confidence.

Dr. Prata: (*To Mr. Sele*) Do you agree?

Mr. Sele: What does it mean "take into their confidence"?

Dr. Prata: It means, if there was a problem . . .

Gino: The first time my father ever talked to me, he put an emotional burden on me. I didn't agree with him, but I didn't know how to get out of it. This was (*turning to Mrs. Sele*) when you hemorrhaged in your eye. I remember the scene, it was quite funny. Mom, naturally, was worried about her eyes. Suddenly she burst out saying: "I don't care about my home or my children anymore!" To me this was perfectly normal, there was the danger that she could become blind.

Dr. Prata: Was it serious?

Mrs. Sele: Yes. It steadily got worse, I was concerned. I don't have the high spirits that I used to have. It could be making them all suffer a bit.

Dr. Prata: You mean, your constant worrying about your eyesight.

Mrs. Sele: It's taken away all my cheerfulness. I'm an optimistic person, but this has been a bit of a tough blow.

Dr. Prata: What were you saying?

Gino: I was 19, and going to the station to catch a train, Dad came with me. He was very worried because he couldn't make sense of Mom's outburst. I got very embarrassed. On one hand I felt he needed reassurance, on the other I saw Mom's reaction as being perfectly normal and justified. These are only flashes I have as far as confiding in us goes.

Dr. Prata: Why did he take you into his confidence then? Was he asking for your support?

Gino: I saw it as letting off steam. I was grown up and so I could be told everything.

Dr. Prata: He could also talk to you about his work? Couldn't he? Whom did he go to if he needed to let off steam?

Gino: He'd let off steam by talking about his problems.

Dr. Prata: With whom?

Gino: To all of us together, at mealtime. Usually we kids could only say: "Why don't you do this or that?" We really weren't qualified to say anything.

Mr. Sele: I always told all of you everything about my life and my work.

Carla: You'd tell us your problems, but you'd never ask us to share them or ask us for advice.

Gino: You'd never touch on any deep problem or feeling.

Dr. Prata: (*To Mr. Sele*) On problems concerning your work, you'd consult them, without asking for advice . . .

Mr. Sele: I'd let them know about things, that's all.

Dr. Prata: Without asking them for their advice. Gino says: "Our remarks never carried much weight."

Gino: Neither Mom nor the four of us ever knew anything about his problems.

Mrs. Sele: It was all technical stuff, how could we have understood it?

Mr. Sele: When I was concerned, they'd say: "Oh come on, don't worry!" This was the kind of support they gave me!

Dr. Prata: Who would Dad tell his troubles to . . . to Mom?

Gino: At mealtime everyone would be present.

Dr. Prata: Was Mom as unqualified as the children?

Gino: Yes, we were all on the same level. Still, the two of them had moments of affection. There was this feeling that Dad might be taking Mom into his confidence. Mom perhaps would be talking things over with him. . . . However, Mom, as a go-between, was in a very ambiguous position. If we wanted to go to a movie, we'd ask Mom, who'd then go and ask Dad for permission.

Dr. Prata: Who would Mom tell her problems to?

Carla: To my aunt who isn't here.

Mr. Sele: To the aunt who runs away.

Dr. Prata: What a shame. Why isn't she here? Does she have the flu or is she running away?

Bianca: Because Aunt Ida doesn't have any children of her own. She's Mom's only sister and considers us like

her adopted children. She acts as if she's our second
mother, she has a lot of influence on our family life.

Dr. Prata: In what way?

Bianca: Inevitably, she influences the rest of the family. Because she has such a big influence on Mom.

Dr. Prata: Does Mom talk more with Ida than with Dad?

Bianca: Yes, I think so.

Dr. Prata: Does Ida's advice carry more weight with you than Dad's?

Bianca: Perhaps, but Dad is thought of as having the sharper mind. My mother's relationship with Aunt Ida is very special.

Dr. Prata: Is Ida the younger sister?

Bianca: Yes.

Mrs. Sele: She's only two years younger than me.

Dr. Prata: How old is she?

Mrs. Sele: Fifty-nine.

Dr. Prata: Are there more phone calls, or visits?

Bianca: Visits, and they have become more frequent lately since my grandmother died. My aunt has attached herself more closely to our family. Besides, now she's retired, with plenty of time on her hands. Also she's taken Maria's problem very much to heart.

Dr. Prata: Before this, only a lot of phone calls from Ida to you?

Bianca: Oh, no, there'd be a lot of visiting, too.

Mrs. Sele: Mainly during the summer.

Mr. Sele: Actually, she lives in Bologna, so while they were at university, their aunt's door was always open.

Dr. Prata: (*To the parents*) Would you go there more often now? When you go to Bologna, do you go to Ida's house?

Mr. Sele: Only every now and then, for dinner! Ida has retired, having lost her parents; she only has a married

	brother. Consequently she comes to us. She's a part of our family, now.
Dr. Prata:	Carla, does this arrangement with Dad as the master mind and this Gulf Stream of confidences flowing to Ida irritate your father?
Carla:	Yes. Mom and Dad don't really see eye to eye on certain matters.
Dr. Prata:	For example?
Carla:	Gino's problems. When Gino stopped visiting us regularly for a while, there was a sort of . . .
Dr. Prata:	A Coral Reef Barrier?
Carla:	Right. A kind of tug-of-war with Alma.
Mr. Sele:	Gino wanted to prove he was autonomous.
Dr. Prata:	Was that in 1973–1974 ?
Carla:	Yes. Mom would have taken a more conciliatory stance, but Dad was adamant. Besides, Mom is more impulsive in tackling problems, while Dad thinks everything twice over before doing anything. Even about Maria and how to handle her. Dad is inclined to play down problems. He breaks it up into parts, whereas Mom gets a bit flustered.
Dr. Prata:	What would he do about problems?
Carla:	I don't know. He'd measure it accurately, scrutinize it, almost too rationally, in my opinion, whereas Mom. . . . .
Dr. Prata:	Tell more about the results of this Pythagorean Theorem. Where did it lead to in the end?
Carla:	To medication.
Dr. Prata:	The neurologist and the medication.
Carla:	No. He wants to find a way to build up her self-confidence again.
Dr. Prata:	Let's go back to Ida, then.
Carla:	When there were these fierce arguments, Mom would turn to Ida for support. There were always

	differences on how to handle things. My aunt was on one side and Dad, considering anything my aunt did as an interference, on the other.
Dr. Prata:	When Ida says something, does it carry much weight with Mom? The two of them tend to agree more often, so on the balance Ida-plus-mother outweighs Dad. Correct?
Carla:	No. They reach a balance, which isn't a balance, really, because my parents are in conflict.
Dr. Prata:	Ah! Dad weighs a lot! Mom-plus-Ida, as a team, makes the score even. Right?
Carla:	Yes.
Dr. Prata:	All this isn't viewed favorably by Dad. It irks him considerably. Right?
Carla:	Yes.
Dr. Prata:	Mom refuses to back down. If she did, she'd find herself very much underweight?
Carla:	Mom won't ever back down.
Dr. Prata:	There's quite a bit of friction between them regarding Ida.
Carla:	Yes.
Dr. Prata:	About what, in particular?
Carla:	About my aunt's interfering with Maria.

(The therapists need a second consultative session and give the appointment to the nuclear family.)

TESTING THE MOTIVATIONS AND EXPECTATIONS OF THE FAMILY

This test should be done at the end of the second session after the therapist has been able to check with the nuclear family the hypotheses he made during the first session and examine any new hypothesis before leaving the children at home (Raffin, 1988; Selvini Palazzoli & Prata, 1982a).

On the other hand, the family needs to know what family therapy really is and what they can expect from the therapist.

One should not take for granted that he has convinced the family of his skills and that the family wants to continue with him. The family may want family therapy, but not with him. Maybe he has been too direct, too boring, too blaming, or even too dangerous for the family's homeostasis. Fair play and strategy suggest that the therapist give them the possibility of saying no and finding another solution.

The Testing of Motivations must be done with the nuclear family. If a member of the extended family or someone else is present in the session, the therapist should accompany this person to the waiting room, telling him that what he has to say to the family is a private matter. Then, when the family leaves at the end of the session, he will shake hands with this person, but must not say a word about the decision they have made. Actually, the *Testing* only concerns the nuclear family, and the conclusion should be given to them only.

Timing is so crucial to our technique that even when the therapist only has the nuclear family at the first session one should always wait until the end of the second session for the Testing.

Let me illustrate the *Testing of Motivations and Expectations* with an example.

The Ansa Family

A family of four from Rapallo, a seaside resort two hours away from Milan, called me in June 1981, for an appointment. Maria, 16 years old, had been anorexic for two years. In spite of her severe loss of weight, only the family doctor had been consulted. He had given her some vitamins and the usual sensible suggestions that always go unheeded. In October, when the family arrived for the first interview, Maria was an ugly skeleton, whereas her sister Cristina was a smart and tanned girl of 18. The parents were a nice looking upper-class couple in their 40s.

The first session was very difficult for me and the second was even worse. The family behaved as if they had been summoned to appear before a court of law. Finally, quite exhausted, I came to the *Testing of Motivations* and the discussion went as follows.

Dr. Prata:	I want to know if you would like to continue these meetings with me and what you expect from me.
Mrs. Ansa:	Doctor, it is very constructive and useful for us to come here, not only for Maria, but for the four of us. I can say that at home talking to each other isn't easy. Time is short. Life is frenetic, and talking is difficult. You must understand, the two hours we spend on the road coming to the center is a nuisance and very inconvenient, especially now that the weather is getting bad. Look at today; we arrived home at one o'clock and were immediately off and running. You know it's very tiring. Just before you came in I had to take some aspirin because of a terrible headache, but don't worry about the headache. It's all right.
Dr. Prata:	And you, Cristina?
Cristina:	Maria refuses to come.
Dr. Prata:	I need *your* answer.
Cristina:	I might come.
Dr. Prata:	And you, Maria?
Maria:	I don't believe in it.
Dr. Prata:	You don't believe in it. Do you have any other solution in mind?
Cristina:	None.
Dr. Prata:	So the best solution, for you, is to do nothing. And you, Mr. Ansa?
Mr. Ansa:	I would like to come. Not only for the family but for the anorexia. I believe in this therapy. If it produces good results, it is appreciated. Anyway, it is up to you. We have discussed this matter at home and there are so many negative aspects. If your center was closer to home, or at least in a more pleasant place, it would be all right. Milan is such a tiring place!

Mrs. Ansa: Half a day is lost in getting here.

Mr. Ansa: If only it could always be spring! There was fog on
                 the way coming here today. However, one must try
                 everything.

Dr. Prata: Now let me go and consult with the team (*exits*).

After these statements, if a therapist prescribes family therapy
and continues working with this family, the therapist is certainly
heading for failure or for an immediate dropout.
We did.
I will give another example of the *Testing of Motivations* in
Chapter 5.

THE SECRET

When using the New Method, a therapist should be extremely
cautious and proceed from one stage to the next after taking into
account all the verbal and nonverbal feedback coming from the
family. One should definitely not treat the parents as candidate
cotherapists before testing them with *the secret* or one will miss the
opportunity to observe their conflicts and record their reciprocal
claims and grudges. The prescription of *the secret* has to remain
cryptic for the parents also. Seldom, when they don't understand
and ask for information, the therapist could explain, briefly, that
the secret concerns everything related to the meeting, everything
that was said and done by them and the therapist during the
session, everything they felt during and after the session.

After telling the parents the prescription of *the secret*, the therapist will give them a paper saying:

• DR. X HAS PRESCRIBED KEEPING *THE SECRET* FROM EVERYONE.

• SECRET NOTES, DATED, WRITTEN SEPARATELY BY EACH OF THE
  PARENTS, WITH THE REACTIONS TO THE DECLARATION OF *THE
  SECRET* MUST BE KEPT.

The parents have to memorize the instructions and then destroy
them. We give that written memorandum to help their memory and

to prevent them from using the ruse of saying they have forgotten or misunderstood the prescription. When a therapist has to face master gamblers, the therapist should remember that naivety only means stupidity.

One asks the parents to announce together *the secret* to the children. Then, in the presence of the children, each of them will phone and announce *the secret* to his/her relatives or significant persons who are aware of the treatment. If someone cannot be reached by telephone, the therapist will ask the parents to visit that person together. The reciprocal control is not hidden at all, even if it is not declared. In fact, when the therapist says: "You will go together and then each of you will note for me the reactions . . . ," one is implicitly telling them to be reciprocal witnesses.

I would like to underline that everything in the New Method is meant to decrease the possibility of maneuvering and cheating. For this reason, it must be followed exactly and without the slightest change by the therapist and by the family. The New Method gives the parents the chance of doing something *together* even before their conflict is solved and before they are spontaneously willing to decrease their escalation. They can work *together* because they have the alibi of the prescription. When the parents have plumbed the depths, they become more willing to change things. Which means, in this case, to change from a sterile arm wrestling to a dynamic tournament between them to see which one of the two will carry out the prescription better.

If they haven't touched bottom yet, they may start competing to see which one will sabotage it better. But since it is a question of *acting* and not of *speaking,* any form of sabotage would soon be discovered. Actually, with the New Method, it is very difficult to cheat.

During the third session and the following one, *after reading the notes written by both parents* as well as asking how the current family situation is and how the I.P. is, the therapist asks how things are going within the couple in order to try and settle the conflict. Nevertheless, one thing must be clearly stated: This is not the matter which has led them to the therapist. The therapist is dealing with them only because he/she needs parents who will collaborate; otherwise they will be easy prey for the I.P.'s secessionist maneuvers. We will thus come back to their mutual claims, but, at that stage, the most urgent thing is to declare *the secret* and jot down all feedbacks. If they get over that test, they will receive other prescriptions that will be difficult to put into practice, which means that they will be forced to try and collaborate as much as possible.

If they follow the prescription, it allows them to come out of a complicated position by breaking the rules of their "game," which they know so well.

The Secret Is Broken

When *the secret* is broken, the treatment must be interrupted by the therapist because one cannot trust the parents either as parents or as cotherapists.

When *the secret* has leaked out by mistake or accidentally, because, for example, someone found the *secret notes*, the therapist must discontinue the treatment because *the secret* is no longer equal for everyone. Consequently, instead of being the instrument for breaking the family "game," it becomes an instrument of reinforcement, making it even more perverse.

If a therapist, for one reason or another, decides to continue the treatment and "see what happens," one should remember this. The parents are not the victims of an unjust situation, but active players of the "game" which maintains that situation. Like master gamblers, they lie in wait for the therapist at each step. When he proves inconsistent with what he has solemnly stated, the parents will stop trusting him. One should keep in mind that each stage of the New Method is a test, a relational and reciprocal test both for the family and the therapist. Consequently, *only after the parents have passed the test of the secret will they become his cotherapists and he become their supervisor.*

When the parents discover that they have broken *the secret* but the therapist does not discontinue the treatment, they will despise him because he is inconsistent and/or is cheating. They have nothing to learn since cheating is their favorite move. The therapist has merely introduced *the secret* as a new move in an old "game," obeying the rules he was supposed to change. From now on, he will have to face any type of reaction from the family members without any therapeutic tools. The I.P. is cheated worse than before in the most unfair manner because the therapist is using a therapeutic context to make a coalition against him.

Therapists usually fear the I.P.'s reaction to the declaration of *the secret*, but the parents never do, since they know their "game" better than we do. What they fear is someone else's reaction. This fear can be so great that they immediately refuse the prescription and drop out. Or, very soon, they will leak *the secret* to this precious "someone," knowing perfectly well that the consequence is the interruption of the treatment.

When the parents phone to inform the therapist that one of them (or both!) have broken *the secret*, an appointment has to be given as soon as possible. The "wait and see" attitude can be, in this case, the most dangerous.

When the parents arrive, and they usually come to the appointed session, the therapist should ask for details, with whom and for what reason he/she has broken *the secret*. What was the reaction of the confidant, the I.P., and the others?

It doesn't matter if only one of the parents seems responsible for the event. Often this is the willing one who is offered to the therapist as the "guilty partner," but the maneuver is frequently a concerted, joint effort against therapy. The therapist, seeing the camouflaged maneuver, can say, for example, with a sad tone of voice, that he understands their feelings but, for fear of hurting their favorite son or a grandmother (who, by the way, has already lived her life), they have destroyed the only instrument he had to cure the I.P. Now, going home, they *must* declare to all the children together that *the secret* has been broken and the therapist has discontinued the treatment.

The declaration will avoid a worsening of the situation. There is absolutely nothing further the therapist can try to do to clarify the situation and stop the "game." Even if the I.P. has already reacted to it with an alarming crisis, I suggest that the therapist resist omnipotent feelings and accept the withdrawal. *This is the best he can do.* Besides, *this interruption* of the therapy is a strong input introduced into the family, a message which could suggest to the I.P. to do the same and leave the battleground.

If the parents immediately refuse the prescription of *the secret*, it is useless to push them. It is better to postpone the therapy and wait until they feel ready. The therapist is also bound to *the secret* and must keep it from everyone. For example, if the referring therapist or a member of the family phones me, I listen to him, ask for information, and possibly tell him something concerning the first two sessions, but *I never reveal anything covered by "the secret."* I say: "I'm sorry. The parents and I have a contract. Like them, I must keep *the secret* from everyone and forever." In the following session, I inform the parents about the call and my answer. There is nothing peculiar in this procedure. Actually, those are the very same rules that all individual and family psychoanalysts must obey.

The third session, as we explained in the New Method, is a structured session. The therapist investigates the way the children reacted to the fact of being left home and the parents being invited alone to the meeting. Then, the therapist asks the parents how *they* reacted to this invitation. *Afterwards*, the therapist can drive his investigation into other directions, as I did in the third session with the Sele family in Chapter 6.

THE DISAPPEARANCES

The disappearances put the I.P. and his siblings on an equal footing and give them a break from too intrusive, omnipresent parents who believe they know what their children think and even what they feel in their hearts and their bodies.

Hundreds of therapists had already failed trying to convince the I.P. to stop lying in bed, playing the watchdog, and to go out, do something. Nevertheless Dr. Selvini and I were trying to devise an intervention which could change the family "game," starting with the I.P.

We understood at last that, to be effective, we needed committed and motivated *parents! They* should be the ones to introduce the "changes" in the family. We devised *a contract* between the two of them and us which could revive that contract of mutual help they had once established when they married, which they were now breaking or cheating on.

The disappearances give the children the opportunity to do something freely, on their own. During the first *evening disappearance,* even grown children stay home doing nothing. The second time they usually organize themselves, phoning a friend, inviting someone to their home, or going out. When the parents *disappear for the weekend,* the children immediately know they have many free hours. They can organize their time and space as they want, and they usually do.

The separation also affects the parents. It gives them the opportunity to stay together alone. When they are in conflict they may agree *to disappear* only because it's a rule, but they will have nothing personal to say to each other. As usual, they will keep speaking of the I.P. If they fear staying alone without the children to mediate their relationship, they will oppose the therapist by presenting a number of difficulties. I listen to their problems, trying to help them to surmount the obstacles. I do not tell them what they should do. I only say how other parents managed to leave their children alone or with a baby-sitter. For example, during the *weekend disappearances,* some parents took the children to another couple, telling them that they needed to go away and leave the children with someone: "Next time we will take care of your children when you go out."

The written message left needs no explanation! There are no deserts around, although some families make their life a desert. However, they can find a way out if they are determined.

Leaving the children alone can be painful to parents who are always in charge of their children. Of everything they do! Maybe the children are in their 20s, but how could the parents leave them alone? Sometimes they are speaking of a 30-year-old son as if he were three years old. They can be so convincing that the therapist can become confused and anxious about leaving the poor helpless thing alone.

To convince such parents *to disappear* is hard work. They can accept the separation only if they are convinced, being the cotherapists, that they are still, and more than ever, in charge of their children's health and future.

I don't believe it when the parents say they feel guilty leaving the children alone. They know they have "problematic children." They know we are trying to solve their problems. When they come out with "guilt," I remind you that guilt is a socially accepted idea, but *control is not*. Don't start saying that you, too, would feel guilty leaving your children alone. You don't have a "psychotic," "anorexic," or whatever child at home. Stop identifying so heavily with the "poor" parents. You would do everything you could for your children, I'm sure. There are no "poor ones" around. But, why don't you try to "identify" with the "poor children" once in a while? Anyway, I don't recommend "identifying" with anyone. There are too many risks involved in the "game."

I say to the parents that they are perfectly free to feel guilty if they want, but they have no reasons for that. They are not "going out" for pleasure; they are *disappearing* to help the I.P. and reorganize their family life in a happier way.

Children should not be left with a member of the family because it spoils *the disappearances* of its greatest meaning and effect. To avoid giving explanations, it's better to call a professional babysitter. Even in the smallest villages, where there are no babysitters available, there is always someone who makes her own living by staying with the sick or old people. My colleagues seem to deal only with parents who have babies! Do they never have primary and secondary schoolchildren as patients? Anyway, I discuss practical and legal arrangements with the parents. If the parents have an only child unable to communicate verbally because he is too young or because he is "autistic," once or twice they could *disappear* with him. He cannot come home and report, for example, to the grandparents where they have been and why.

When a member of the household lives with the nuclear family, it partially spoils *the disappearances* of their effect *on the children* because they will not remain alone. That family member could be persuaded to go on a vacation or pay a visit to someone. Sometimes it works. As before, *the disappearances* will be effective as an *input* into the family system when a member of the extended family lives next door in the same building or is very enmeshed with the nuclear family.

I remember a family of four where the firstborn was a 10-year-old girl. Her sister, seven years old, had been labelled as psychotic (Selvini Palazzoli & Prata, 1982a). The family had just moved to a new house in the country which was isolated and unfinished. Dr. Selvini got upset: "How can the children be left alone in that house without even a railing on the stairs?" I said: "Look, Mara, if you go back to the parents with all these problems in mind, you will certainly convey to the parents the analogic message that you give a prescription which is impossible to follow. Give the prescription and if *they* raise a problem, *then* you can discuss it with them. Don't anticipate doubts and problems." She prescribed the *evening disappearances* and the parents accepted it without objections. For the *weekends*, they found a retired lady who had been their maid before the children were born.

When the parents are willing to collaborate, they always find a solution. The first feedback we obtain from the prescription is the parents' reaction. Children's and the extended family's feedback follow, giving us information that would have taken years of nonprescriptive family therapy to uncover. We have to rely on parents' *notes* for the feedback. As I said, the therapist is responsible for the therapy, but he is not responsible for the correct execution of the prescriptions. When one has been careful and clear in one's explanation, as soon as the parents have agreed to follow the prescriptions, they become the responsible party. Sometimes we worry too much. Then, when we prescribe the *disappearances*, we discover that the parents see it as an opportunity to experience the adolescence they missed.

When the parents do not accept the prescriptions or drop out, we would investigate their reasons. Then we analyze the case, trying to discover our mistake and find out what we missed. Listening to the tapes, as I always do, I discover, for example, that I said valid things using a wrong tone. In other cases, I was too pedagogic or too insistent. The tone we use is extremely important because we can hit the target but lose the family when we use a wrong tone.

The supervisor plays an extremely important role, controlling not only what the therapist is missing but also how he is conducting the session (Bateson, 1972b). Looking for "mistakes," we also read their *notes* and our summaries again, those we wrote after each session, and discuss the case with the team. Very often we discover that we had noted and *written* an important fact which we then completely forgot.

Before each session, we read the chart and the underlined passages of each summary. We don't run from one session to another.

If we did, I am sure we would make a lot of mistakes and learn nothing. Mistakes can be the best teachers for a therapist, but one should not overindulge in them.

POOR FAMILIES AND THE DISAPPEARANCES

In the U.S. and Canada, where I have been invited to run workshops, the lack of money becomes the insurmountable obstacle for *the disappearances*. I believe that the problem arises more in the mind of therapists than in the family.

In Europe, even very poor families always find a solution and manage to disappear. For example, in 1983, an extremely poor family of five from Southern Italy came to the center. They looked like an advertisement for poverty and bad luck, a sort of "Rocco and his brothers" family. The parents, old and sick, were almost unable to read or write. The father had recently had pneumonia and the mother was debilitated with rheumatism. They told me that they couldn't afford to disappear right now because they had spent all their money treating their 18-year-old anorexic daughter. I said, "Never mind, you don't have any money left. Wait until September, then phone and tell me if you have found some money and feel ready to leave for a month. If not, don't worry, I can wait and give you this prescription in October, November, or whenever you are ready *to disappear.*"

I gave them a telephone appointment and they left. I received a call from the mother 10 minutes after I arrived home: "Dr. Prata, my husband phoned a friend and asked him for a loan. So, we don't have to wait and phone in September, you can give us an appointment right now because we already have the money!"

"Madam, I don't want to push you; take your time!"

"Doctor, why are you making such a fuss? We have the money and we can go!"

They spent the summer in Southern Italy with the I.P., their other two married children, and the extended family. Then, on August 16, as soon as the caravan arrived home, they entered their apartment, left *the message* in the kitchen, and disappeared for a month.

When they returned home, their hysterical, chronic, despotic "anorexic" daughter was "cured!" She had menstruated and found a job as a baby-sitter. She also had met a boy from Southern Italy. A year later she was married and two years later she had her first child. The parents graciously phoned me saying how happy and grateful they were.

Another very poor family of four had a chronic anorexic daughter. The parents found at each stage of the prescription a funny solution for their lack of money. They went into a chicken coop for their *evening disappearances* and spent four hours there, in the dark, with some wine, sandwiches, and . . . 50 chickens. I almost died laughing when I heard that.

For the *weekends,* they took the car and left home on Friday evening until Sunday night. They drove to the next street, where a relative had a summer house. They had the key and just moved 600 feet from home. They put the car in the garage, took some food and candles, and spent three weekends with the windows and the shutters closed. They were so contented when they related their adventure that I assumed they were making love most of the time.

Another poor couple rented a tent and two bicycles, and *disappeared for three weeks.*

Since we do not live in the middle of nowhere, I believe that when a family really wants to follow the prescription they find a solution.

The Sum Family

The prescription of the disappearances was given at the end of the fourth session to the Sum family, a family of four. *Henry,* six years old, was an "autistic" child. His "striking" sister, Francesca was eight years old. At the beginning of the session, the parents and the therapist listened to the recorded voice of Henry speaking and singing for his third birthday. Six months later he became "autistic" and since then had not spoken a word.

Conclusion of the Fourth Session—June 5, 1982

Dr. Prata: So you have been able to follow the prescription of the secret.

Mrs. Sum: Without difficulties.

Dr. Prata: Good, but you were prepared for even more demand-
                ing questioning. *The secret* was a test to verify if it
                would be possible to go on with the next prescrip-
                tion. We have treated children in worse situations
                than Henry's with our method, but I have to give
                tiring and difficult prescriptions.

Mr. Sum: Difficult for us?

Dr. Prata: Yes. Now you are Henry's therapists 24 hours a day
                under my supervision. I will tell what you shall do.
                The next session will be in six weeks, on June 22 at
                4:30 P.M. All right?

Mrs. Sum: We will be in the country, but even if we were on
                the seashore . . .

Mr. Sum: Doctor, remember that we will not make problems.
                Sea or mountains, we will come in any case.

Dr. Prata: Fine. I will be expecting you. My prescription of *the
                secret* remains the same, but now there is a more
                difficult task. At what time do you usually have
                dinner?

Mrs. Sum: At 8 P.M.

Dr. Prata: And you, when do you return from work?

Mr. Sum: Usually between 6:30 and 7 P.M.

Dr. Prata: Mr. Sum, I need you to do the following: During
                this six-week period, four times, instead of coming
                home, you should wait for your wife somewhere,
                because disappearing from home without being no-
                ticed is more difficult for two than for one. You
                have to organize yourself and then go out even if
                there is an unexpected visitor. You will do this four
                times.

Mr. Sum: Yes.

Dr. Prata: Mrs. Sum, at 7 P.M. your husband will not return
                home and you will go out to meet him. You will leave
                home before dinner and without preparing any food.

Mrs. Sum: And the children? I have to leave them alone?

Dr. Prata: Yes, I'm sure that they will find something to eat in the fridge. You will leave a message twice written by you, Mrs. Sum, and twice written by you, Mr. Sum, without any signature. Leave it in the kitchen. In order to help your memory, I wrote it here. The message is *"Tonight we are not here."*

Mrs. Sum: Fine. How long should we stay out?

Dr. Prata: Come back at 11 P.M.

Mrs. Sum: (*With a sigh*) Oh, God!

Dr. Prata: From 7 to 11 P.M.; it's a prescription very difficult to follow and it's such a source of anxiety. But so many words have been spent on Henry that it's time for action or he will not come out from his "autism." Now I will tell you the prescription and then you will tell me if you feel that you can do this or not. At seven you leave your note and meet your husband. This prescription will be more difficult for you, Mrs. Sum, but once or twice you, Mr. Sum, should go home earlier. Let your wife leave and then you leave.

When you return home at 11 P.M., the children will ask you, if they are awake, or the next day: "Where have you been? What have you done? Why did you desert two poor children? Are you crazy?" To their questions and to those of everyone else, you will answer: "These things concern only the two of us." Do not mention Dr. Prata. These things must come out as if they were settled by you. Then, I need *the notes* that each of you will write separately about the reactions to your disappearance. Hide *the notes*, because the children usually do become curious. Even the most quiet one will start searching in your bag, in the drawers, for something to explain what's going on.

I oblige you to give the same explanation to everyone and write (with the date) the significant reactions to your disappearances. Granny Maria will probably phone Henry and Francesca. Francesca

will tell her: "They went out." "Do you know where
they are?" "There is a message." Maria will tell you
that you are crazy and Dr. Prata, too, if she suggested such a reckless thing. You will answer:
"Those things concern only the two of us" in your
dialect. It will be more natural.

Mrs. Sum: I will do this even if I am extremely anxious because
I never leave the children alone.

Dr. Prata: I know. They will react to that and you will write
down their reactions. *The notes* are not to be a secret
between the two of you, but you will write them
separately and read them to me. Each of you will
observe different reactions, changing moods, irrita-
tions, questions, and so forth. When reading your
notes, we will have a more detailed picture of the
children, of Maria, of your parents' reactions. Even
the priest . . .

Mrs. Sum: The priest has nothing to do with us!

Dr. Prata: Anyway, write the notes and keep it secret!

Mr. Sum: Four disappearances.

Dr. Prata: Yes, four in six weeks. You will have to organize
that.

Mrs. Sum: Ah! Four times in six weeks! I thought four times a
week!

Dr. Prata: No, no!

Mrs. Sum: I am afraid of Henry going out!

Mr. Sum: We could lock the door.

Dr. Prata: Certainly.

Mr. Sum: We'll shut off the gas, too, and the water.

Mrs. Sum: Henry could reopen the gas.

Dr. Prata: Francesca will be there and we will see how she
intervenes if Henry does something wrong.

Mrs. Sum: Today I left them at my mother's country house, in
our apartment. I told Francesca: "Francesca,

Granny Elsa will come to have lunch with you, but you have to pay attention to Henry because of the tractors, the river, etc." "Don't worry mum, I will do everything. I will change him, give him his suppository, everything!"

Dr. Prata: But when you *disappear,* you will not give her any information, with words, with your eyes, or even with your eyebrows. You will even go out without makeup. Just open the door and leave when they are in the toilet or in their bedroom. They will only find the message. I am not interested in what you do outside. If you like, you can tell me. The point is that you have to go where no one knows you.

Mr. Sum: The only reactions will come from the children. The others will not come or call.

Mrs. Sum: They will probably phone in six weeks, and your mother will come to see Francesca and Francesca will inform her. We will go to see my parents and Francesca will tell them.

Dr. Prata: "You are crazy, don't you read the newspapers? There are plenty of kidnappings, houses on fire, burglars!" I know that I am asking you to do something heavy, but Henry's situation is serious and it is difficult to get him out of it. We absolutely need to do something and the only way out is this. You are the therapists. If you don't feel like completing this prescription just as I said and you are tempted to ask the next door neighbor to look after the children "because you have to go out for Henry's therapy," it is better to wait. You only say the agreed sentence of *the secret* if you don't feel like taking the next step.

Mrs. Sum: We will take it.

Dr. Prata: You can stop now and keep *the secret.*

Mr. Sum: No, we will do exactly as you said.

Dr. Prata: Well. On Tuesday, June 22 at 4:30 P.M., we will meet again, the three of us. You have some time left to organize yourselves.

Mr. Sum: Psychologically.

(*They take leave, shaking hands with the therapist cordially.*)

THE WRITTEN MEMORANDUM

1. Concerning *the secret*
   * DR. X. HAS PRESCRIBED KEEPING *THE SECRET* FROM EVERYONE FOREVER.
   * SECRET NOTES, DATED AND WRITTEN SEPARATELY BY EACH OF THE PARENTS, WITH THE REACTIONS TO THE DECLARATION OF *THE SECRET* MUST BE KEPT.
2. Concerning *the evening disappearances*
   * A WRITTEN MESSAGE: "WE'LL NOT BE IN TONIGHT."
   * TO MAINTAIN *THE SECRET,* AVOID GOING WHERE SOMEONE MIGHT REPORT YOUR WHEREABOUTS.
   * *THIS CONCERNS ONLY THE TWO OF US.*
   * *SECRET NOTES,* DATED, WRITTEN SEPARATELY BY EACH OF THE PARENTS, WITH THE REACTIONS TO THE *EVENING DISAPPEARANCES,* MUST BE KEPT.
   * DO NOT INQUIRE ABOUT WHAT HAPPENED DURING THE *DISAPPEARANCES.*
3. Concerning *the weekend disappearances*
   * A WRITTEN MESSAGE: "WE WILL COME HOME ON SUNDAY NIGHT, LATE."
   (Obviously the parents can choose any moment of the week to stay out two nights).
   * (The following passages of the MEMORANDUM will be the same.)
4. Concerning *the long disappearance*
   * A WRITTEN MESSAGE: WE WILL COME BACK ON . . . ," etc.

When the children are young, a baby-sitter will "appear" on the appointed day of the long *disappearance*. It should not be shorter than a week. The baby-sitter should receive a secret envelope with a telephone number where she could phone in case of emergency.

Obviously, when we are dealing with teenagers, nobody will come to take care of them. In this case, the *disappearance* should be of 21–30 consecutive days.

If need be, when a grandfather or a grandmother is ill, the parents are allowed to phone the doctor for news without letting him know where they are.

4

The Second Session

THE SELE FAMILY

Second Part of Session Two—September 11, 1985:
Parents and Children

Dr. Prata: Now I would like to hear everyone, beginning with you, Mr. Sele, tell me your reasons for coming and what you expect from family therapy.

Mr. Sele: Well, I'll be frank: I don't know enough about it. So I'm a bit skeptical. I would do anything in the world for Maria, to see her calm, contented, and happy again. I sought help where I thought I might find it, I have asked friends about it, and some said this and others said that . . .

Dr. Prata: Was it Gino's idea?

Mr. Sele: Yes. It was mostly Gino's. Naturally, having a son who is a physician . . .

Dr. Prata: Was it Gino who insisted?

Mr. Sele: Well, yes, all right. I'd do anything to . . .

Dr. Prata: What do you expect this therapy to do?

Mr. Sele: I hope it works. The important thing, as far as I'm concerned, is for Maria to get back to being the way she was six years ago. She was the most highly regarded girl in the family. She was wise, worked hard, had such perseverance and willpower. Especially when Gino disappointed me so, I shifted all my expectations onto Maria, who was the wisest of them.

Dr. Prata: And all these are things you've lost now, haven't you?

Mr. Sele: Yes. And I've made many sacrifices in order to have her return to . . .

Dr. Prata: Would you be more in favor of family therapy or individual therapy?

Mr. Sele: I don't know, I trust Gino's judgment and yours. I'd make any sacrifice!

Dr. Prata: What about you, Mrs. Sele?

Mrs. Sele: Oh, I'm an ignorant person.

Dr. Prata: Well, are you interested in doing family therapy, or aren't you?

Mrs. Sele: I think it'll work better than individual therapy in Maria's case, because she has never really accepted psychotherapy. She had gotten rather fond of her individual therapist and . . .

Dr. Prata: That's beside the point! Do you wish to do family therapy? Are you for or against it?

Mrs. Sele: I'm in favor because I think it might be less upsetting for her.

Dr. Prata: And as to your expectations?

Mrs. Sele: Well, I expect to get some advice on how to behave towards her. Also whether we should have her go and see someone who'll prescribe some medication.

Maria: My mother thinks I have a biological problem. There has been a coincidence of different periods happening in February, and so she thinks it's something that happens in springtime, something biological.

Dr. Prata: Let's go in order of birth: Gino, you made the inqui-
                ries, you pushed all of them to come here. If you had
                not insisted, would they have come here?

Gino: No! And I had to use a little pressure on Maria.
                Actually, she wasn't and she still isn't enthusiastic
                about it. . . .

Dr. Prata: So, you are quite in favor of this kind of therapy.
                What are your expectations?

Gino: Immediately, to try to unblock this tension that has
                been created around Maria.

Dr. Prata: Who has created this tension?

Gino: Mostly, our parents, who are living through the
                highly traumatic effects of this problem. It helped
                bring them closer together, but now they feel it is
                very harmful.

Dr. Prata: It brought them closer together?

Gino: As a couple, they were united in their anxiety about
                what to do with Maria. . . . Their attitudes differ on
                this point. . . .

Dr. Prata: But what do you expect from family therapy?

Gino: I expect family therapy to unblock this tension cen-
                tered around Maria. The atmosphere at home . . .
                has been getting very heavy. Very tense! So my ex-
                pectations center on releasing this hypothetical
                block that's keeping Maria tied up in some way.
                Also, an attempt to find a satisfactory way out for
                Maria and for all of us.

Dr. Prata: I see. Let's hear from Maria, now. Do you favor
                family therapy and, if so, what do you expect it to
                do?

Maria: Well, I'm certainly not going to have any more indi-
                vidual therapy. That's for sure (*weeps*)! I don't know
                about family. . . . I was very doubtful when it was

suggested, because I took it to be an excuse for everyone to air his or her own personal problems.

Dr. Prata: When did you think this? Before or now? I want to know what you think today!

Maria: About coming here, they said that it wouldn't be only for me, but also for Carla and Gino and the others.

Dr. Prata: That's true.

Gino: Last time we were here, I gained a few flashes of insight into my life. Things I'd never thought about before. So, I, too, can find something helpful for myself, here. . . .

Dr. Prata: All of us can have trouble relating. . . .

Maria: I don't know.

Dr. Prata: Going back to my question, Maria, would you be interested in coming to family therapy or wouldn't you?

Maria: I'd like to know exactly how long it would take. First. And . . .

Dr. Prata: I told you there would be 10 sessions at most, with an interval of one month between sessions. We've already done two of them, so that leaves eight, if we were to go on with it.

Maria: (*Still weeping*) Well, yes.

Dr. Prata: All right. And your expectations?

Maria: I can't bear this state of uncertainty any longer. So, never mind the whole mess, and all the psychoanalysts on earth, I simply must find a solution. If you believe I can find a solution here, of course I suppose there can't be a full guarantee.

Dr. Prata: You're shifting the question back to me. What I want to know is, what are your expectations?

Maria: To be able to make a decision, once and for all.

Dr. Prata: About your future?

Maria: Today's session has made me think that I'll . . .

Dr. Prata: Stop sitting around waiting for esteem, appreciation, and love to come your way?

Maria: So, my only solution is: No matter what kind of work turns up, what I have to do is to get away from home.

Dr. Prata: Are you asking for help in leaving home? (*Silence, weeps*) Leaving home at the age of 30 is nothing to cry about! Let's go on to Carla. What do you think about family therapy and what do you expect it to do?

Carla: As I see it, family therapy could clear things up. Lots of things have been said, or thought of, but never in the presence of each other. That's what makes it interesting, a bit risky, perhaps. Surely there will be problems and the relationship binding each of us to the others might start hurting, but it could be pleasant and provide useful stimulation.

Dr. Prata: So, you would be in favor.

Carla: Yes. Regarding Maria, I don't know in what way . . . Maria usually expects solutions, practical suggestions. I don't know if many of those will emerge here. Suggestions are like brief flashes. The solutions she'll have to find for herself. She's been through other types of therapy and she's already discarded a number of suggested solutions, but those may have been the wrong kind of therapy, and this could be the right kind. She'll have to be the one who wants to come, though, and not just wait until . . .

Dr. Prata: Please, Carla, stop sermonizing and playing the big sister!

Maria: That's something I have been saying to her ever since February!

Carla: Nevertheless, I'm always the one most . . . Maria has set me up as her touchstone, and my parents have saddled me with this birthright thing. It's all very provoking.

Dr. Prata: Carla, you rather enjoy it, don't you?

Carla: Not at all!

Maria: Oh come on!

Dr. Prata: Maria is dying to get hold of this birthright! Don't attempt to brush it aside. The fact is that she, the second born, was skipped over. Besides, the fact that you came third but have now overtaken her in terms of esteem and expectations is a source of humiliation to her. So, the birthright may entail certain duties and burdens, but it's also highly gratifying. Let's not look at the burden aspect because this hot potato of birthright is something that makes those who don't have it feel very bad indeed.

Mrs. Sele: If really there is such a thing as this birthright, we didn't take it away from Maria. It was she who wouldn't do . . .

Dr. Prata: Anyway, for one reason or another, the fact remains that it passed from Gino to Carla. Now here's Bianca coming up from behind to receive it, and Maria finds herself bringing up the rear.

Mr. Sele: For me, Maria will always be the firstborn, right after Gino, despite all the problems.

Dr. Prata: A rather moth-eaten firstborn, no?

Mr. Sele: Oh no, even the way she is I accept her . . .

Mrs. Sele: As long as she's willing to listen to us . . . when we ask her for advice, she gives it and we listen to her, so . . .

Mr. Sele: As long as she doesn't act stubborn.

Dr. Prata: "Just so long as she listens to what we say." This is different from your attitude with Gino, isn't it? . . . As a matter of fact, he does entirely as he pleases. Carla, too, has lately been doing what you expect

	her to do. She is making sacrifices regarding certain aspects of herself, but she, too, is able to do a few things for herself. So, it seems to me that this idea of "Just so long as she does what we say" crops up chiefly around Maria. Concerning Bianca, perhaps, but since Maria is 12 years older. . . . Well, Bianca, as to family therapy what are your expectations?
Mr. Sele:	I hope I wasn't misunderstood, when I mentioned that I'd been advised . . . if a friend of mine says: "Look, your daughter needs this particular medicine," I try to persuade her to take it, and she must take it.
Dr. Prata:	Maria would first have to be convinced that she's ill, and *she's not ill*! Bianca.
Bianca:	I'm in favor, because a lot of things have surfaced here and a lot of others will that are important to know. I was struck by the things that have emerged. Many times I could tell in advance what they were going to say, but, as I see it, my parents, have never said a lot of these things before. Certain things have never come out into the open. As for my own expectations, well . . . mainly that this problem of Maria's will become less dramatic. The whole family, and she, too, will manage to tone it down. Maria will acquire more self-confidence and she'll stop considering it to be a problem. . . .
Dr. Prata:	What problem are you referring to?
Bianca:	I mean, stop thinking of it as an illness. . . .
Maria:	When you say: "Maria's problem" you are labelling me as a patient, though you may not be aware of it.
Bianca:	No, I told you before, that in my opinion, you're not ill; it's just the way you behave.
Dr. Prata:	Maria's mad as a hornet about a whole lot of things that are unfair, or that she considers unfair. There's no point in putting a label marked illness on some-

	thing that's simply a vendetta. There's nothing biological!
Bianca:	Well, but when Maria drives me up the wall, going on about her troubles, you can't help saying she's sick because . . .
Dr. Prata:	No, she is a nuisance. A hell of a bore. That's what Maria is.
Maria:	Well, when I ask you to tell me about your problems, all you do is shut me out!
Dr. Prata:	Bianca, would you say that your expectations might be that Maria will get rid of this idea that she's . . .
Bianca:	. . . a patient.
Dr. Prata:	. . . and that she will solve her problems herself?

(*Dr. Prata exits.*)
(In this family, the parents were motivated and the referring sibling was not *that* "prestigious one." Family therapy was prescribed and the parents came alone to the third session. See Chapter 5, p. 125.)

THE PROTI FAMILY

Second Session

Apparently this family was living a more dramatic situation than the Bar family (p. 46), but the "game" was the same. Playing the gentle husband and the "omni-understanding" father, Mr. Proti had won his children and his mother-in-law over to him. Mrs. Proti had already seen the maneuver after the birth of her first daughter, Valeria. She refused to have other children, but Mr. Proti insisted so much that Mrs. Proti agreed to have a second baby. She became extremely attached to the new child, but little by little Mr. Proti also succeeded in drawing the second daughter, Nerina, to himself. He was so "sweet and gentle . . . and absent!" that Mrs. Proti was unable to find a direct way to express her anger. She tried the "unfaithfulness" move, which failed. Then she became "depressed" and made the "hypochondriac move." Then came the "alcoholic move" and finally the "suicide move," all with negative results. The more difficult Mrs. Proti became, the more of a "saint" and "victim" was Mr. Proti. When the family arrived, Mr. Proti was a slim, calm, and collected man. Mrs. Proti, who had been a beautiful woman, was fat and bloated. Valeria, a nice girl, looked very much like her father, while Nerina, blonde, smart and simpática, resembled her mother.

Referring person:	Mrs. Proti's physician.
Who called:	Mr. Proti, on October 14, 1986, for his wife who has been depressed for eight years.
Initial diagnosis:	Depressive neurosis.
Place of residence:	Milan.
Father:	Fabio. Age 47. High school diploma. Head manager in an import-export company. He travels considerably, mainly to foreign countries, often staying away for a month or two. Birthplace: Napoli.
Mother:	*Wilma.* Age 39. Grade school. She would like to find a job but can't. She has been depressed for the past eight years. Housewife. Birthplace: Milan.
Date of marriage:	August 11, 1963.
Religion:	Roman Catholic.
Other members of the household and their relationship:	None.
Children in order of birth:	
Valeria	Age 21 (May 3, 1964). She is working for a degree in Fine Arts (painting).

Nerina	Age 18. Simpática, not very studious but she got a high school diploma. Presently looking for a job.
Father's family:	*Father* died before Mr. Proti was born. *Mother:* Giovanna. Age 67. Lives in Taranto. She remarried. *Her second husband* died in 1970.
Mother's family:	*Father* died some years ago, when he was 65, of a heart attack. *Mother:* Daniela. Age 75. Lives two blocks away from the Protis. She would occasionally come to help Wilma. There are *two sisters*, married, with children living in Milan. They never come to visit.

Problem

Wilma started suffering from depression eight years ago after a hysterectomy. She had wanted Valeria, the first daughter, and tried to avoid the second pregnancy. However, when Nerina was born, Mrs. Proti began to adore her, saying that Nerina was very much like her while Valeria resembled her husband. Mrs. Proti explained her original refusal of the second child, saying that she hadn't wanted to take away her affection from Valeria. After Valeria's birth, Mrs. Proti had become anxious and extremely concerned about subsequent pregnancies. She was having many problems with her uterus, nauseas, and pain.

All the medical findings were negative. Her uterus had only a small imperfection. After the uterus was removed, Mrs. Proti began to complain about her intestines, saying that she was sure she had cancer. Again the medical exams proved negative. She began Freudian analysis, "but the analyst was too cold and unfriendly." Mrs. Proti left him and subsequently discontinued therapy with two other analysts as well. She tried "group therapy" and "couple therapy" without any result. Finally, she began to tell the children that she wanted to commit suicide. Several times she opened the window and attempted to throw herself out while Mr. Proti held her down.

Then Mrs. Proti attempted suicide by slitting her wrist. She had to be hospitalized twice for a month. She accuses Mr. Proti of committing her to the hospital, when in fact *she* asked to be hospitalized. She is now under medication. Her state has improved, she can go out and drive, but she has become openly hostile and aggressive towards her husband. The original telephone call to the center was made by Mr. Proti, but Mrs. Proti had pushed him to phone. She even called him at work to check if he had asked for an appointment.

Invited to the first session: the nuclear family.

Summary of the First Session—October 26, 1986: Parents and children.

The members of the family seemed to confirm the "Withdrawal of Significant Ones" hypothesis. By the end of this session, we understood why Mr. Proti spoke in such an indirect way, being cautious and carefully splitting hairs. Soon after birth, he had been entrusted to his paternal grandparents and concealed as an illegitimate child. His mother very seldom visited him and kept his existence a secret from her second husband and in-laws.

He grew up in a village where he was never allowed to express himself sincerely. His family let the neighbors and schoolmates think that he was the only son of his widowed mother who had remarried. However, it was absolutely concealed from everyone that he knew nothing of his mother's new family and, in Taranto, where she lived, no one was aware of his existence. Moreover, the maternal grandparents never clearly explained to him how things were. They always referred to him in a circumspect way.

We could infer that Mr. Proti, feeling very insecure, had always behaved as a good child without any protest and never did create problems because he was too afraid the grandparents would reject him. He would then be lost since his mother had virtually repudiated him. This hypothesis proved correct. In this learning context, he became cautious, swallowing the bitter circumstances, "forgiving" in order to avoid being chased away. Valeria seemed to have decided to side conclusively with her father against her mother.

She appeared pedantic, circumspect, with a personality too rigid for her age.

Mrs. Proti comes from a completely different learning context. Her sister, Bruna, a sickly child, had become the favorite of their mother, an ignorant woman who preferred screaming to talking. Mrs. Proti was openly her father's favorite. He was an intelligent, educated, and interesting man, but confronted with his wife and Bruna, he was a loser. The alliance with Wilma was not helpful to him. Wilma, like her father, was excluded from a relationship with her mother and desperately longed for it. Both of them exhibited their "second best privileged relationship," trying unsuccessfully to provoke the winner's attention and jealousy.

Wilma's father, because of his discomfort and loser's rage, had tried the "economic failure," "depression," and "alcoholic" moves in the family "game." The results he obtained were just the opposite of what he had expected: He was even more rejected and despised by his wife. Mrs. Proti had learned from her mother to be extremely direct and to express herself with screams rather than conversation. She had learned from her father to resort to "depression" to express her unhappiness and have the upper hand. Did she also resort to alcoholism? Probably. Mrs. Proti was convinced that screaming was the winning move. Concerning "depression," she had probably come to the conclusion that *she could do better than her father and win.*

But it did not work for her.

Nerina, a beautiful teenager, resembled her mother physically and psychologically. She constantly resorted to the "I don't remember" move to avoid being engaged. By refusing to side with one parent against the other and trying to understand both of them, Nerina had acquired a finely tuned personality—more attractive than Valeria's. This seemed to make her more vulnerable and unhappy than her sister.

Summary of the Second Session—November 26, 1986: Parents and Children.

When the family arrives, all of them look more cheerful and more relaxed. Valeria and Nerina are less heavily made up than when they were in the first session, as if prepared to let themselves go and express their feelings. They say that they have not given much thought to the last session because Mrs. Proti had an attack of biliary colic that kept her in bed for a fortnight. Now she is no longer taking drugs, is slimmer, and better dressed. During the past two weeks she has been living an almost normal life.

In our opinion, her last bout of depression, the one that made them seek therapy, was and still is connected with the fact that Nerina, formerly deeply attached to her mother, appeared to be falling under her father's influence, like Valeria. Mr. Proti had held "four family sessions" at home: three to try to get Nerina to share the housework and one, last night, to clarify the role of each member of the family.

Mr. Proti:	It became clear that, of the four of us, three were playing a definite role.
Dr. Prata:	Which three?
Mr. Proti:	Valeria, Nerina, and I.
Dr. Prata:	What roles?
Mr. Proti:	(1) I am the economic bastion, providing security and protection; everyone in this family knows whom to turn to if there are problems. (2) Valeria looks after the house. As such, she has become, probably unintentionally, a mother substitute, and not merely in practical terms. My wife said something highly characteristic: "I feel like a daughter."
Dr. Prata:	What is Nerina's role in the family?
Mr. Proti:	(*Smiling affectionately*) She is the brazen girl!
Dr. Prata:	She refuses to play the mother like Valeria!
Mr. Proti:	Absolutely.
Dr. Prata:	Mr. Proti, you say: "The three of us have a role to play, but my wife hasn't got any."
Mr. Proti:	My wife wouldn't even dream of having one.
Mrs. Proti:	(*Sounding fatuous*) Mine is a rather different role. But then I am always plagued by my lack of self-confidence.

Dr. Prata: I was interested to hear that you don't have any role.

Mrs. Proti: I don't have any role when I feel poorly. Then I take a black view of things.

Dr. Prata: You are a mother who looks on the black side, but you don't stop being a mother at that point!

Mrs. Proti: Yes, that's true. I used to be an active, constantly involved, ever-present mother, at a time that my daughters may no longer remember (*in a sad voice*).

Dr. Prata: Did you feel like playing the role of the wife as well?

Mrs. Proti: Yes, I did, then.

Dr. Prata: And of the woman?

Mrs. Proti: Yes. But then I got ill.

Dr. Prata: Full of sadness, of discontent.

Mrs. Proti: Indeed, but I also wasn't up and about.

Dr. Prata: And so you had to give up the role of the active mother and assume that of a mother on relief. And what about the role of woman and wife?

Mrs. Proti: When I fell ill, the wife's role turned into a tragedy because, and my daughters know it, my husband and I had no sex for eight years. Since I lack self-confidence, that was the straw that broke the camel's back.

Dr. Prata: Was it because of your uterus that you didn't have sex?

Mrs. Proti: No, when I fell ill, my husband went through a spell of impotence, that is, he couldn't get an erection.

Dr. Prata: As a reaction? Let's see which came first, the chicken or the egg.

Mrs. Proti: There were no sexual relations, but there was also no emotional contact of any kind. Still, this last month we have been talking more to each other and we have also had sex on three occasions.

Mrs. Proti claims that all her troubles are bound up with her husband's having given her a hard time as a mother, as a wife, and as a woman, so much so that her hysterectomy brought her no relief. The only way in which she could regain her self-esteem was to have an affair, but her lover had also been impotent, as well as alcoholic. Mr. Proti had made his wife pay dearly for this betrayal and not until after the last session had he found it in him to say, "I forgive you." But the family "game" had not really been changed. There had been just one difference: Previously, Mr. Proti used to say, "I shall never forgive you," and Mrs. Proti would retort: "How long will I have to pay for it?" Now Mr. Proti says, "I have forgiven you," and Mrs. Proti replies: "I don't believe that you *really* have."

Mr. Proti:	I always thought our relationship was solid, I was convinced that she would never play me false.
Dr. Prata:	And so the betrayal hurt you in two ways.
Mr. Proti:	Indeed it did.
Dr. Prata:	Inasmuch as you had been rejected, hidden away by your mother.
Mr. Proti:	But I was already the forgiving one.
Dr. Prata:	Yes, but then, it was like a burn on an already scorched skin.
Mr. Proti:	Yes, it was the same old story, but this time enacted by someone I had chosen myself. I didn't chose my parents after all (*in a martyred tone evidently meant for the children*).
Dr. Prata:	Now we can understand why you have been so heartless to deprive her of Nerina for three whole months. Your wife took her revenge for your disdain with a love affair. You, Mr. Proti, took yours by spiriting her three-year-old daughter away and by not forgiving her until a month ago. Your wife came to hate you even more and you made her pay for it. What we have here are two interlocking vendettas and you two were prepared to carry on with them all your

	life. I think you have already done each other as much harm as you can.
Mrs. Proti:	No doubt about that.
Mr. Proti:	Terrible harm. It was like a road accident.
Dr. Prata:	Yes, one in which both of you had your faces smashed. Now that we have taken stock of the situation, it must have become obvious to both of you that there is no point in continuing the vendetta. My suggestion is to bury the past, but not in the sense of driving it into the unconscious or the subconscious, or by beating about the bush. Let's just bury it for good. It's been such a sad business! Like a plane with the brakes on that revs up its engines as hard as it can but never takes off. So, you know what my suggestion is.
Mrs. Proti:	Yes, I accept it wholeheartedly.
Dr. Prata:	You have had a terribly difficult life. If you have any pity for yourselves and for each other, then just say enough is enough! Make sure that the future is more tolerable because so far your life has been sheer hell.

At this point I put a question I always ask the children during the second session, first to Valeria and then to Nerina: *"Considering your parents as a couple, whom do you consider the winner and whom the loser in this marriage?"* For Valeria the winner has always been her mother, not least because, of the two of them, her father was more in love. For Nerina, her mother had always been the loser, though now she seemed to be gaining the upper hand. However, she felt they both needed each other and there was a strong bond between them.

Mrs. Proti confirms that, despite everything, they have never spoken of a separation. Nerina reveals that, a year ago, her mother had another love affair, something that deeply upset the entire family. She (Nerina) did not want to be involved any longer, and that is why everybody in the family accused her of being an egoist. As far as Mrs. Proti's drinking was concerned, it appeared that she now drank very rarely, though only a year ago she had always walked about the house with a bottle of whisky in her hand. I gathered that she did most of her drinking in the evening when the whole family could see her and try to stop her.

Mr. Proti: (*In a martyred voice*) From 1978, it was I who took care of the house. I cooked, did the shopping, and so, being the practical psychologist, the odd-job man, the cook, the nurse, etc. . . . I forgot about being the husband, about even being a man. If we had found the right person at once, we wouldn't be here.

Mr. Proti is very shrewd: he presents his marital shortcomings as the direct result of the sacrifices he has had to make, and so he is "one up" once again. He then does a bit of wheedling in order to win the therapist over to his side.

The question: "*Whom do you consider the winner and whom the loser?*" is followed by: "*Whom did you used to side with and whom do you side with now?*" (Prata, 1988, pp. 113–132).

Valeria, copying her father, tries to present herself as a "perfectly good and generous person," one who has always gone out of her way to make her mother see her father's point of view. Instead of receiving praise, she was treated like a fool by the therapist.

Dr. Prata: At 21, you can't be this gentleman's and this lady's mother.

Valeria: What I am worried about is my future.

Dr. Prata: Because you like playing the little mother.

Valeria: Yes, sometimes I can accept it quite readily.

Dr. Prata: Never mind accepting it, what I want to know is if you are prepared to drop it. The more you do that, the more of a mother she is likely to become again.

Valeria: So I should drop it?

Dr. Prata:	Absolutely!
Valeria:	(*Very shrewdly*) We'll have to see what my mother thinks.
Dr. Prata:	I don't care two pins about that. Your mother might even ask you to carry on. . . . What I am saying is that there has been nothing positive in it for you and nothing positive for your mother, either. When a daughter assumes and clings to the role of being her own mother's mother, then the hierarchic levels are stood on their head and the real mother is put "down." Even when she asks you to carry on playing the mother, simply because she is in the habit of asking you to, and you are foolish enough to swallow the bait. You pay dearly for it though you may like it. That role is unproductive for everybody and there-fore the more quickly you drop it the better. . . . Your mother may ask you to continue, but she cer-tainly realizes that being her 21-year-old girl's daughter is a putdown for her. Is that clear?
Valeria:	Perfectly.
Dr. Prata:	And you, Nerina, whom do you side with?
Nerina:	(*Crying*) I feel utterly helpless, I don't know what to do or what to say.
Dr. Prata:	Of course not, because, in hierarchic respects, you are not meant to be your parents' mother. It's already drained Valeria, more fool she. It's no wonder you feel helpless. That's because on the hierarchic level you are the daughter. Go and look it up in the Regis-ter of Births and Deaths, you were born so many years after them and so many years after their mar-riage. It's not you who brought them to the altar and so there is no sense in your trying to cope with their marriage.
Mrs. Proti:	Not with the marriage, but with my crisis!
Dr. Prata:	Look, Mrs. Proti, your crises are much more bound up with your marital life.

Mrs. Proti: If I am to be abandoned by everyone, by my mother, by my relatives, by my daughters, and by my husband, then I simply can't go on living.

Dr. Prata: No one has been talking of abandoning you. But the more your mother, that great critic and blamer, washes her hands of you, the more thanks you should give to St. Lucy! As for your sister, who has you so much under her thumb, the more she keeps to her own home, the better it is for you. I have merely been trying to tell Valeria and Nerina that if they revert to the role of daughters it will be much better for you and your husband.

Mrs. Proti: I live in fear of being left alone.

Dr. Prata: Mrs. Proti, come on! Your daughters are quite right to say that there is a strong bond between you and your husband.

Mr. Proti: Yes, we have come to realize that.

Testing the Motivations and Expectations of the Family

Dr. Prata: Today we must come to a decision about the therapy. I need to know if you, Mr. Proti, want family therapy. True, the final decision will be taken by us, but we need to know what you think about it.

Mr. Proti: I "personally" want to continue.

Dr. Prata: With what expectations?

Mr. Proti: I'd like to get a clearer picture of our relationship because I am worried that after a moment of euphoria we may fall flat on our face again. I don't know what I should do for the best or what they should do.

Dr. Prata: By "they," you are referring to your wife?

Mr. Proti: The girls as well, because they have to stay with us for a few more years. I am convinced that, for better or for worse, we have managed to build up a family with strong bonds, one in which there is a chance of talking things over. I don't have much time to spare because I haven't managed to find a way of earning a living that keeps me less busy. (*Mr. Proti is uttering economic threats.*) At the age of 50, it is difficult to change jobs. If I stop earning money, then all of you will have to work; that suits me fine, I'll gladly stay at home!

Dr. Prata: You said, in fact, "I want to reach a better understanding, because my relationship with my wife is difficult and with my children as well." Mrs. Proti, do *you* want family therapy?

Mrs. Proti: Yes. Not only because of family problems, but also because I hope that these discussions may help me to gain the self-confidence I lack. That means trying to improve my relationship with the rest of my family. I want to live a peaceful life.

Dr. Prata: Valeria?

Valeria: I am all in favor of continuing these discussions although I felt I was not personally involved in family therapy anymore.

Dr. Prata: But what are your expectations now?

Valeria: Above all, to be able to settle our family situation and see the hierarchy restored. I want to feel more tranquil and I think that if certain problems were solved we should no longer have all her aggression erupting from time to time. Yes, I'd like to continue these therapy sessions.

Dr. Prata: Do you expect anything else?

Valeria: An improvement in their relationship because, over the past 10 years, all they have done is to be at each other's throats. They haven't lived like husband and wife.

Dr. Prata: They didn't even live properly as human beings. And you, Nerina?

Nerina: Like Valeria, I didn't think there was any need for me to return here. All the same, I am in favor of carrying on because, quite apart from the problems between the two of them, there are problems involving the whole family and because I hope that therapy may help to turn us into a normal family again.

Dr. Prata: And perhaps you also hope to rid yourself of the label of egoist. I shall leave you now. I'll be back in two minutes.

I leave and then return saying that the team had decided that there are indications in favor of family therapy. Next time the two girls will stay at home and the parents will come alone. The leave-taking is cordial.

In this family the affective *Withdrawal of Significant Ones* hypothesis was accurate. The New Method proved effective, especially since the children became less family-oriented and got engaged.

Mr. Proti's business trips to Hong Kong made the intervals between family therapy sessions much longer than the usual months (Selvini Palazzoli, 1980). That is why we held three sessions with Mrs. Proti and twice we suggested that she "disappear" for 10 days and go to a health spa to take care of herself. She drinks only occasionally, she never speaks of committing suicide, and, having lost 22 pounds, she looks much better.

5

The Third Session

THE SELE FAMILY

Session Three—December 10, 1985: The Parents Alone

The therapist opens the session by asking the parents for the children's reaction to the fact that they were left home and the couple was asked to return alone. Then the therapist inquires about everybody's reaction following the last session and about any comments that may have been made prior to the current session.

Mr. and Mrs. Sele assert that Gino, Carla, and Bianca considered it quite normal that their parents should have been asked to attend by themselves, each of them coming up with some explanation. Maria, on the contrary, had a very negative reaction. She disqualified the therapy, saying that it did her no good and, worse still, that it threatened to "unhinge their family life." In addition, she told her mother how to behave during the session. "Don't you dare talk about medication! And don't talk about sex either, just get down to brass tacks." Maria was furious because, according to her, not only had there been too few references to her during the first two sessions, but on top of that she was now being left behind at home. Consequently, last month, Maria's symptoms aggravated.

The therapist concludes the series of questions centered on the children's reactions, summing up what had arisen during the first part of the interview and making Maria's behavior explicit.

Dr. Prata: . . . I'd say she's done everything possible to discourage you from coming here. (*Mrs. Sele mumbles feeble*

125

> *denials.*) She stated very clearly that she doesn't want to study. She wants to work, but she spent the last few days in bed. All of this has to do with your coming here . . .

Mrs. Sele: Yes, but . . .

Dr. Prata: Anyway, she's doing all she can to discourage you from attending therapy sessions. This is quite obvious to me.

Mr. Sele: Yes, she keeps flaunting her skepticism.

Dr. Prata: Perfect.

Then the interview centers on the parents' reaction to their having been asked to attend the session without their children. The therapist turns to Mr. Sele first. As it happens so often in the third session, marital problems emerge immediately; the expectations reflect the couple's hope that a solution to their problems will emerge, not merely to Maria's problem. Mr. Sele has not forgotten Maria's statement during the last session that Mrs. Sele had confessed to her that she had married him without love. Mr. Sele is patently anxious to find out if that statement was true. His insistence that his wife could not have been serious, and that there must be alternative explanations, suggests that he is not at all certain about his relationship with his wife.

The therapist hands this implicit request for clarification directly on to Mrs. Sele, who claims that she made the remark only to help Maria! The therapist intervenes to define the parental prerogatives: "It's none of the children's business whether or not their parents were in love when they got married!" However, she lets them understand that it is not clear why Mrs. Sele chose this kind of information to help her daughter. Why, exactly, did Mrs. Sele tell that story to Maria? There is good reason to suspect that by making her daughter privy to her marital dissatisfaction she was trying to turn the girl against her father. It is important to establish how Mrs. Sele feels about her relationship with her husband. Moreover, a discussion of her love life, assumed or real, is likely to give rise to interesting transactions. Hence, the therapist insists on asking Mrs. Sele whether or not she is in love with her husband.

In fact, the picture Mrs. Sele draws of her married life is rather gloomy. She has never been in love with him, but would never be unfaithful. He has squashed her psychologically.

That declaration triggers off a series of reactions that not only highlight the couple's mutual dissatisfactions but also bring into the open other facts, such as that following Aunt Ida's suggestion, a psychologist was consulted about all educational problems; that Mr. Sele was kept in the dark about the children's pranks, and so on, all of which gives the therapist a clearer picture of the family's relational "game."

Dr. Prata: Just a minute, Mr. Sele. Concerning the children, therefore, matters of sex were not the only things that were concealed from you. There were also petty pranks.

Mr. Sele: Yes, so I wouldn't get upset and react too severely.

Mrs. Sele: But I didn't even know he had stolen an electric train!

Mr. Sele: Oh yes, you knew it, you'd hidden it behind the books so I wouldn't see it.

Dr. Prata: And did you find it?

Mr. Sele: No. I may be ironfisted, adamant, too finicky, but I've always been absolutely open and trusting. My family tried to shield me and keep things from me that they knew would upset me, partly because I suffered from heart troubles, partly because I was so exhausted by my work, and partly because I wasn't that close to my children.

Dr. Prata: Who did your wife conspire with, to be able to hide these things?

Mr. Sele: With Ida, I guess.

Mrs. Sele: Nonsense, Ida had nothing to do with anything at that time.

Mr. Sele: Well, one thing I was sure of was that, if we got onto the subject of our relationship, we were going to have an argument, but anyway. . . .

Dr. Prata: What?

Mr. Sele: I see things one way, and she another, so . . .

Dr. Prata: You were going to have a squabble here, or at home?

Mr. Sele: Here. . . . A lot of delicate things were to come up, a conflict of opinions.

Dr. Prata: So, you feel that the children oppose you. Your wife follows her sister's advice and is a bit against you, too.

Mr. Sele: Yes, it's what I keep saying. It's what I've said during the fights we had these past few days.

The therapist's final question to Mr. Sele—*"Do you feel your children are against you? Does your wife take her sister's advice and tend to be against you as well?"*—is the enunciation of a hypothesis which the therapist now proposes to check, namely, that her parents' disagreements and Aunt Ida's interference, which has surfaced several times, have turned Maria increasingly against her father, causing her to adopt those very attitudes that displease him: sexually provocative habits and a failure at school.

The second part of the session is devoted to testing this hypothesis, beginning with an attempt to establish whether or not Aunt Ida has been playing an "instigative game" (Selvini Palazzoli, 1983). The therapist's precise questions help to overcome Mr. Sele's reluctance to admit that he considers his sister-in-law's presence in his family life an intrusion. Mr. Sele mentions an episode that clearly shows up Aunt Ida's instigation. It is just one of the examples that both members of the couple now mention, as if they had suddenly grasped the real nature of an uncomfortable situation they have been aware of for years but have been unable to fathom.

The idea of an "instigative game" seems to have been confirmed and the therapist now feels able to explain her hypothesis. The various pieces of information she has gathered during the sessions, starting with the items recorded in the telephone chart, can now be fitted together in a logical and significant way (Raffin, 1988; Selvini Palazzoli, 1986).

Dr. Prata: In your opinion, what influences does Ida have on the children, and especially on Maria?

Mr. Sele: First of all, she keeps us informed of what is happening and is more liberal in her thinking. The girls think they'll find a more sympathetic attitude in Ida than in me because I take a more austere attitude.

Dr. Prata: Well, if it's only a matter of whom one confides in, that's not so important. . . . But don't you have the impression that Ida is pitting Maria against you?

Mr. Sele: No.

Dr. Prata: Well, *I do, and very much so.* In my opinion, there's a very serious threat from Ida, who is instigating Maria against you.

Mr. Sele: That could be, but I can't really imagine it. If Ida does, she doesn't mean any harm.

Dr. Prata: I don't really care if she means any harm or not! When symptoms continue for such a long time, my experience tells me that it isn't just something that grows out of a single angry moment or out of resentment over some unfair behavior on the part of the parents. Or because one of the parents has shifted his or her alliance from the identified patient to someone else. This type of thing can provoke a desire for revenge and anger. We've talked quite freely about that here.

These things last for some time and if no one fans the flames it gets back to normal. One can take a year or two of revenge because one feels betrayed either by Dad or by Mom. But eventually, one leaves it at that. However, if all this continues and requires taking to one's bed and doing nothing. . . . For instance, in this case, Mr. Sele is obsessed with school and sex, and Maria puts him on the rack with her behavior regarding school and sex. Gino told me

	on the phone that Maria had taken the pills after two big rows with her father.
Mrs. Sele:	I'm sure it was that way the second time.
Mr. Sele:	The second time, yes. The first time no. That was a surprise to me, too. I had cancer and was hospitalized . . .
Dr. Prata:	The truth is that your daughter is out to make you pay through the nose, even if it means ruining her own life.
Mr. Sele:	Really?
Dr. Prata:	And in this—however good or bad her intentions may be— there is a lot of complicity and instigating by Ida. In my opinion, there's no doubt about it.
Mr. Sele:	Definitely. I entirely agree with you and, if you wish me to, I'll go into a lot of details, now that you've made me think of it. Honestly, it hadn't occurred to me before. For instance, my not giving the children enough money brings up comparisons made by Ida: "My brother gives his children pocket money." So I ended up giving Carla and Bianca a monthly allowance. . . . Then there's this business of me demeaning my wife with her salary. Ida keeps on criticizing me for being too tightfisted, too interested in money matters, in worldly goods, in the family fortune; Ida would like to manage our property against my wishes.
Dr. Prata:	Fine. A lot of things can come to light, as we go on. Mrs. Sele, do you agree? Even the children have confirmed this "instigative game." Ida probably plays this "game" with all the children, but especially with Maria, and she found a sympathetic ally in you. She is pitting your daughter against your husband.
Mrs. Sele:	Not openly, though. Although it is true! I remember something now, Maria got involved with a ne'er-do-

well; she was dating a baker's boy, can you imagine anything like that!

Dr. Prata: The reason she might go to bed with a streetsweeper or a greengrocer's boy was to make her father suffer. So she demeaned herself not because of a "weak ego" or a "weak something else." What was it? *"The emotional sphere"*? She does it simply because, by debasing herself, shacking up with the most disreputable person she can lay her hands on, is tantamount to cutting off one of her father's limbs.

Mrs. Sele: This happened when she was 18. There's been this festering sore for 12 years. After that, Maria had another affair and then another. She probably took Ida into her confidence: "I'm a real whore, I'm not right anymore." This was when Ida, seeing Maria wasn't well at all and crying her heart out, advised her to go into group therapy. Maria told me she was the only one in her group who would weep during psychodrama sessions.

Dr. Prata: No! You're changing the subject. My question was: Do you feel that Ida is . . .

Mrs. Sele: No, no, she isn't! I can assure you that my sister always says: "Your husband mustn't know, because Maria feels guilty precisely because she knows *he would never forgive her.*"

Dr. Prata: Look, Maria does all these things to hurt her father and you, Madam, what do you do? You cover up for her, so her father won't know!

Mrs. Sele: But what on earth should I have done, then?

Dr. Prata: I understand how you feel. She's your oldest daughter, but Maria is on the warpath, plotting her vendetta against her father because of a number of things that happened. There are a list of grievances she feels she has suffered. So, she jumped into bed with a swineherd to hurt her father very effectively.

You, in good faith, don't even tell him! This makes it necessary for her to go further. She must debase herself even more until finally her father knows it all.

Mrs. Sele: I found out about this four years ago.

Mr. Sele: Look, there's no point in your trying to. . . .

Dr. Prata: (To Mrs. Sele) All right. There's an escalation. First Maria goes to bed with Tom, Dick, and Harry, next the greengrocer's boy, and after that someone still lower down on the scale. Finally, she gets all the way down to Franco, who's absolutely rock-bottom. . . . Really, if that isn't rubbing it in, until finally the matter comes directly to her father and he gets it right smack in the solar plexus. Madam, you are always ready to put a patch on everything. What Maria wants, as a result of her botching everything, is for her father to see that he's made a mistake.

Mrs. Sele: What mistake?

Dr. Prata: Dad simply did *everything wrong*, because he took a hard line, lacking flexibility and so on.

Mrs. Sele: But who . . .

Dr. Prata: Maria wants to bring this into the open, but behind her, egging her on, there's Ida.

Mrs. Sele: Ida blames herself because one day, while chatting with our maid, she said Maria had gone to her teacher saying that her father didn't love her. He only loved Gino. Ida wasn't sure whether or not Maria had overheard this conversation.

Dr. Prata: I'm quite sure that Ida had been signalling her total disapproval of your husband to Maria in a number of ways and for a long time through her whole attitude, by raising her eyebrows, sighing, and so on. When Maria started acting the way she did, with her father as her target, although lots of it was aimed at Mom as well, she had Ida supporting her.

Mrs. Sele: Ida was minding her own business . . .

Dr. Prata: That's where it all comes from. Otherwise it would
               have ended in one or two years' time. The fact that it
               is festering to make someone pay for what's been
               done to her is because there's someone fanning the
               flames. . . .

Mr. Sele: Well, what shall we do?

Dr. Prata: Either we undo this or things will go on this way for
               as long as you live.

Mrs. Sele: It's a very delicate matter; Ida will be terribly upset.

Dr. Prata: You'll have to choose. I'm not asking you to do any-
               thing against Ida. Your sister has lived her life,
               whereas Maria has all her life to live. You should get
               your priorities straight and make a decision. You
               brought me a problem to solve, which started a long
               time ago. This problem is getting more gangrenous.
               At this point, not only is your husband under fire but
               Maria has nicely managed to get the two of you to
               squabble; she's wedged between the two of you.
               You've taught school for so many years and you
               surely recall that age-old trick of "divide and rule."
               The Romans knew it; the enemy is much easier to
               defeat if you can split him into separate warring
               factions. . . .

Mrs. Sele: It's a perfectly unconscious thing on her part. It's
               only because her whole life is given over to Maria!

Dr. Prata: Let's leave the unconscious out of this! These things
               are done quite openly. The proof is, Maria is hop-
               ping mad because I've uncovered a whole lot of
               things. I've dealt out plenty of hard knocks to both of
               you, but not enough to please her. What I should do,
               in her opinion, is side with her completely, declare
               that you are wrong, and knock your heads together,
               that's all. She noticed that I pay attention to relation-
               ships, that I'm trying to discover what *she*, too,
               might have done wrong and I've fallen out of favor

with her. I'm a hard nut to crack. So the important thing is for you to avoid this trap of the "divide and rule" strategy. Because the "rule" isn't aimed only at Dad. Once Maria manages to play the two of you against each other, she can conquer both of you. There's also the problem of defusing Ida. I'm going out to discuss this point with the team.

Mr. Sele: There's just one thing. Ida has always had a problem with me, but I'm quite sure that she doesn't act this way out of spite. She doesn't mean to set my family against me. She does it because she never listens to what I have to say and always finds some excuse for this. I could go on ticking off a long list of things, "One sells one's property to help one's children, whereas you're not doing a thing for Maria!"

Mr. Sele: Oh well, this was something she said. . . .

Dr. Prata: I see it as being every bit as harmful as poison. This is a well-placed dart of criticism: "You don't do a thing for your child . . ." (*to Mrs. Sele*). You're very attached to Ida. She is so intelligent, she is liable to say things that make you think: "My sister might be right." But, what happens? The result is that you are pitted against your husband, Maria against her father, and, last but not least, you two are split apart.

Mr. Sele: When Maria was studying for her examinations, she wanted to be with Ida, who spoiled her with chocolates and the like, but Maria'd get at Ida in a way in which I, with my heart as heavy as it is, would never have done.

Dr. Prata: Ida will get caught in the undertow sooner or later, because whoever gets "instigated" isn't likely to be grateful to the "instigator.". . . When someone's been egged on and becomes powerful, he starts enjoying his power so much that he crushes everyone underfoot, including the "instigator."

Mr. Sele:	She's already started giving Ida the cold shoulder. This hurts Ida so much that she weeps from morning to night.
Dr. Prata:	So we've reached the stage of power for power's sake (Russell, 1938). We've got to find a way to head this thing off.

(Dr. Prata exits, then reenters.)

Conclusion of the Session

Dr. Prata:	The only chance we have is to use a prescription we used back in 1979 in serious and delicate cases such as yours. This is the way it goes: First of all, you will come alone to the next session. Our therapy is based on secrecy—there will be other prescriptions, but all of them will be based on keeping everything secret. When will the entire family be at home?
Mr. Sele:	On Saturday. Gino will call this evening and ask about the session. He'll be visiting us on Saturday.
Dr. Prata:	Do we have to wait until Saturday?
Mr. Sele:	Yes. I don't trust my wife at home alone with the children because the girls are so clever at wheedling information out of her.
Dr. Prata:	*(to Mrs. Sele)* The point is whether we're to do surgery or put a piece of gauze on an open wound. I know, it's very hard on you because of your rapport with Ida, but you must make a choice *(the therapist reads the prescription).* "Dr. Prata has prescribed to us to keep *the secret* from everyone and forever." You're not to provide any sort of explanation; it's to be somewhat cryptic. You're to announce the prescription of *the secret* when there are as many of you as possible gathered together. I attach the utmost importance to the fact that both of you go together

and tell Ida about this. *All you have to add is that the next session will be on Tuesday January 7th, 1986, with the two of you alone.* The sooner you go and see Ida together, the better.

Discussion of the Session

The precision with which the relational "game" has been mapped out and the fact that the family itself has come up with a host of confirmations make for an incisive intervention, so much so that it is promptly accepted by Mr. and Mrs. Sele, who prove ready and motivated to pursue the therapy and to accept the prescription of *the secret*. At the end they were committing themselves to working out solutions that would render the prescription of *the secret* as effective as possible.

Summary of the Fourth Session—January 7, 1986: The Parents Alone

Mr. and Mrs. Sele arrive with detailed notes about *the secret*. There had been one slight upset: While Mr. Sele was typing the notes the day before, he had been surprised by Maria, but he reacted quickly and gave nothing away. Maria left him with the idea that he was writing notes about household matters.

As for the reactions to *the secret:* While Aunt Ida and Bianca seemed able to accept it without too much curiosity, Gino and Carla insisted that their mother give them a personal account of her feelings about the session. At first, Maria withdrew into her shell, without saying a single word. Then, during the night she made a noisy scene, verbally assaulting her mother, accusing her of betraying her trust, and threatening coarsely to gas the whole family before committing suicide herself.

The parents' reaction had been firm and correct. Carla then sprung to their defense, playing the role of the older sister. Mr. and Mrs. Sele reported that Carla's arrogance had so irritated Maria that she locked herself in her room and spent the following day in bed.

This month, Mr. Sele and Bianca had been very busy helping Gino move and clearing up a family-owned apartment in Bologna.

That apartment was meant to be for Bianca. All the children had lived there in turns while going to the university, and Maria was very attached to it. She reacted furiously and refused to help. Therefore, the session centered on the hypothesis that Maria was protesting against an economic injustice in favor of Gino and her sisters. Mr. and Mrs. Sele deny that she is protesting her property rights, but admit that Maria is incensed at Carla's avidity, arrogance, at her knack of acquiring presents, clothes, and so on, and at her misappropriation of any nice things Maria owns but does not use. It turns out that Mr. and Mrs. Sele often intervene between the two sisters, acting as if Maria were a small baby unable to stand up for herself. The "birthright" which Carla has wrested from Maria seems to have slipped into Bianca's hands. Carla lost out to Bianca when her old "fiancé," a divorced man, developed serious intentions. That was sufficient to lose her parents' esteem. However, the "birthright" is still out of Maria's reach.

The Seles appear to follow a fixed script: Every time one of the children finds a partner, he/she loses his/her parents' esteem. It happened to Gino and Maria, and now to Carla. But now Bianca's exceptional beauty, charm, and intelligence seem to weight more and more in her favor. Hence, it is possible that Carla's more demanding attachment to her parents and her playing the role of Maria's older sister are bound up with her fear of losing her place. Despite this fact, however, Carla and Bianca have formed an alliance against Maria, though each of them interferes in the other's relationship with the parents, and especially with the father.

Mr. and Mrs. Sele's marital relationship has greatly improved during the past month. This has been the only positive aspect of a period beset with difficulties and illnesses.

The therapist then prescribed four *evening disappearances,* one of them possibly in the absence of Maria, to show everyone that they were not meant only for her, and one in the presence of Gino.

After that session, all further contacts were by telephone. Mr. Sele asked to postpone the next session because his physical condition had deteriorated. The doctors suspected a metastasis of a tumor which had been removed and the whole family was very worried about him. Mr. Sele telephoned again a month later to say that he had had an operation and had only a few more months to live. Maria was looking after him in every possible way and in the most affectionate and efficient fashion at that.

After the summer, Mr. Sele telephoned to say that his condition had deteriorated further and he could no longer leave his bed. Maria's apathy had vanished and she was looking after him and the house to lighten her mother's task. She had done well in her studies and had won a competition. She had become engaged to a nice young man, a graduate who came from a good family, and was talking of about getting married. Her parents were encouraging her.

Mrs. Sele telephoned in March 1987 to say that her husband had died at the end of December. Maria got married at the beginning of March and was well. Mrs. Sele was worn out from caring for her husband; his death had shaken her badly and her eyesight had deteriorated even further. Now she would like Carla and Bianca to get married as soon as possible so that she could reorganize her own life and live like an elderly lady who needs peace and quiet.

Follow-up

Dr. Prata telephoned Mrs. Sele on October 22, 1987.

The last session—the fourth—had taken place in January 1986. Mrs. Sele seemed pleased with the telephone call; she felt overwhelmed by all the duties she had had to shoulder after Mr. Sele's death. Gino and Maria were very well. Carla had a good job and wanted to marry her fiancé. Bianca was doing well in her studies and was engaged. All of them had suffered a great deal through Mr. Sele's death; he had been a strong person and had looked after each and every one of them. Mrs. Sele and the children had greatly admired his serenity facing pain and death. His long agony had left everyone exhausted. Fortunately, Maria had got married and that had turned out to be a good thing. The entire family was well and felt no need to go to other therapists. Their positive evolution was confirmed.

6

When the Therapist
Should Say No

After concluding the exploratory phase, the team could decide that the best thing to do is to refuse the therapy. This intervention is dramatic for the family and also for the therapist. But "dramatic" doesn't necessarily mean "effective." To hit the target, this intervention must be systemic and prepared in detail.

FIRST EXAMPLE

The heavy enmeshment of a grandmother into the nuclear family life had become evident. Besides, the therapist had unmasked an "instigative game" (Selvini Palazzoli, 1983) played by that grandmother with a member of the third generation with the complicity of a member of the second generation (one of the parents) against the other parent. The therapist here can conclude the session saying that family therapy is needed but, for the moment, it's impossible "because the grandmother would suffer too much if the relation changes and she feels thrown out."

This conclusion is a time bomb. The first explosion occurs in the session room. The "accomplice" parent and the "instigated" grandchild will try in every possible way to negate the existence of such a "game" and oppose the therapist's decision. For example, the "accomplice" parent could retort: "It's too easy to say that family therapy is needed but is impossible to apply. Be honest! Say that you are unable to treat our case!" Or something of the kind. However, they have to surrender to the proofs the therapist has collected during the exploratory session. The "game," once discovered, will become more difficult to play.

The second major explosion will occur at home. The members of the family against whom the "instigative game" is played will be so infuriated that they could succeed in "throwing the grandmother out" and changing the "game."

With the passage of time, we can expect the family to phone, asking for a session. The therapist can collect information regarding the events following the session and the family situation at present and then decide with the team if it is better to give an appointment to the nuclear family or to let them wait for a certain amount of time.

SECOND EXAMPLE

Sometimes, the conflict within the couple, "open" or revealed by the therapist, is particularly virulent. In this case the therapist could refuse therapy, saying, for example, that the parents would be too emotionally disturbed if the children would become psychologically autonomous and leave them to themselves when they are in such a painful disagreement (Prata, 1983a; Stanton, 1981).

If a stronger intervention is needed, the therapist could tell the parents that, in his opinion, they are totally unprepared to loose the children because they are the clubs they use to beat each other. Family therapy would be too risky for them because the children could withdraw from the combat, leaving them totally exposed in their conflict.

In this case, too, before refusing therapy, the therapist should have irrefutable data as proof when the contest occurs because, even when this intervention is done with empathy, without any accusatory tone, the parents will reject being told they are using their children as clubs. The children will oppose being reduced to the rank of clubs when they were convinced that they were playing an active and important part in the family "game." When they return home, they will decide what is more convenient for them: to continue playing the same "game" or to look around and find someone else to play more lively "games."

In my opinion, when the children are present, any intervention pivoting on the parents must be used very seldom and only as an "extrema ratio" (Prata, 1983b).

On the contrary, when family therapy is under way and the children are at home, nothing forbids the therapist to tell the parents they are "using" their children to hurt each other.

THIRD EXAMPLE

It's technically more effective and systemically more correct to hit members of the first and/or third generation. At the Lyon's Congress in 1982, I presented *The Family "O"* case (Prata, 1983a). The audience consisted mainly of "Love and Concern Therapists." The intervention on the attractive and moving adolescent son of the disastrous conflicting couple provoked an uproar. Consequently, after facing the obstinate contest of the family, I had to face the irate contest of the audience. Many of these screamed that they "wanted to strangle me for my cruelty." They would have cried with the alcoholic mother, patiently waiting for the father to reveal his soul's secret. They would have encouraged the son to continue being the "peacemaker" between his parents and invited his sisters to do the same and help him. Granted! Family therapy was not feasible because the father and the two girls were not motivated. But . . . each member of the family should have had an individual therapist for support.

In my opinion it would have been dangerous because, as in most conflicts, "the more people who enter the arena, the more dead and wounded one can see."

The follow-up I made three-and-a-half years later proved that our intervention had been effective. Mrs. "O," the I.P., had stopped drinking, was no longer depressed, and had started working. Mr. "O," immediately after the session, went to live with the mistress he had had for years and whom, in agreement with his wife, he had hidden from us. He had asked for a legal separation and then for a divorce. The "peacemaker" son had friends and a fiancée and was going out with them. The two younger sisters were following their brother's example, becoming more autonomous and sociable.

It is excessive and not systemic to kill a therapist before he has "produced" the follow-up.

FOURTH EXAMPLE

At present, I always use the "refusal of the therapy" when the person who brings the family to the therapy is a "prestigious sibling" (Selvini Palazzoli, 1985a). In this case, the conclusion must be given to him, obviously in the presence of the family. I say: "Family therapy is especially recommended in this family situation. (*Pause*) But we can't do it because you (*name of the "prestigious sibling"*) could run the risk of becoming even more depressed than (*name of the identified patient*) if through the therapy you lose the position you have in your family." And so on.

The "prestigious sibling" has pushed his family to family therapy. Now, we refuse it because it's dangerous for him. Obviously, the therapist will have to face a merciless contest from the "prestigious" one, from the parents, and from the other siblings. Only the identified patient will react as if he had received a sudden illumination. He may show it only on the analogic level, but he has perfectly understood the meaning of the intervention and is silently in agreement with the therapist.

THE MINA FAMILY

The Mina family will help me to illustrate *how to refuse therapy and how to face the contest which follows* (Selvini Palazzoli, 1985a, 1986). (Their Telephone Chart was given as an example in Chapter 2, page 30)

Second Session—December 10, 1985: Mrs. Mina, Her Four Children, and Aldo, Carla's Husband

Aldo had been invited to the first session and also to the second. As a rule, he should have been dismissed at the end of the first session. But, indeed, the "Prestigious Sibling Game" is peculiar and difficult to uncover. Ciro, the I.P., was living with him and

Carla. We wanted to understand the role Aldo played. Was he supporting or opposing Carla's "paterfamilias" role?

Anyway, we needed his presence to check our hypothesis and uncover the "game." If the "Prestigious Sibling" hypothesis proved wrong, we would accompany him to the waiting room before giving the conclusion. If our hypothesis proved correct, it would have been extremely profitable to have him witness the conclusion. Undoubtedly, Aldo was involved in the family "game." Hopefully, he could help Carla to disentangle herself from it. In this instance, the "game" would change and the family situation would be reshaped.

The Testing of Motivations and Expectations was too long and articulated to be reported here. In synthesis: Mrs. Mina and Aldo declared themselves ready to follow Carla's advice. Carla and Anna were definitely in favor of family therapy. Marco and Ciro, the I.P., were against it.

Conclusion of the Session

Dr. Prata: Carla, since you were the one to ask for therapy, I will give my answer to you. Our team has had a long discussion and came to the conclusion that there are indications in favor of family therapy. (*Pause*) But we can't do it.

Carla: Why not?

Dr. Prata: Because you aren't ready for it. By virtue of very unhappy family circumstances, you, Carla, have been forced to assume a role which wasn't "a filial role." As you put it: "I've had to be the *paterfamilias*." It means that you have been placed in a higher hierarchical position than your siblings. You can feel the growing burden of your role, but you also feel that it gets you a great deal of respect and prestige within the family. And so you are loath to give it up.

Carla: Because the loss would be too sudden?

Dr. Prata: You would like to get rid of the "heavy" bit, but you want to retain your position over your siblings, your role of *paterfamilias*. That would suit you fine, but unfortunately the two aspects are inseparable. And so, despite the indications in favor of family therapy, we cannot proceed because right now you are not yet ready to renounce that role.

Carla: How will I be able to tell when I'm ready to telephone you again? What must I do?

Marco: You aren't ready.

Carla: Right, I'm not ready, but what can be done in this kind of situation?

Dr. Prata: I can only tell you how we view matters today, based on what you have been saying during these two sessions. Perhaps the others had been hoping that once you, Carla, got married, their turn would come to weigh more in the family. In the event, you did get married but only made your presence in the family felt more strongly. It is impossible to get rid of the burden and keep the power that goes with giving advice and being listened to.

Ciro: I'm going out for a moment.

Marco: You stay here!

Dr. Prata: Ciro, I have finished. It's a very heavy crown.

Carla: It has its price.

Dr. Prata: Yes, it weights you down but . . .

Carla: But I like it!

Dr. Prata: Yes, you like it. You want to hang on to it. That makes everyone in the family feel uneasy.

Carla: No, not while I prove adequate to the task.

Dr. Prata: That's not the point. With the passage of time, your responsibility has become greater and greater. But even if it causes a rift in your marriage, you won't allow any of the others to be a competitor. At first because they were too small, later because they were adolescents, but now they are adults! Still, you are so convinced that you are the only one capable of shouldering responsibility that you have become like the patriarch Abraham, who carried everything on his shoulders. You are not ready to renounce your role of seeing to things and being the great provider, because you find that role most gratifying, even if you have to pay dearly for it.

Carla: So all the trouble in the family will end if I abdicate?

Mrs. Mina: What about the practical side?

Dr. Prata: Precisely, when you, Carla, abdicate. But it will take at least six months before you are ready for that. I can see that you are very upset, there are tears in your eyes, you feel the weight bearing down on you, but you still love to run the family. You invited Ciro to stay in your house, with the result that the others . . .

Carla: They won't agree.

Dr. Prata: They never take any responsibility because you take all the decisions half an hour before they even think of them. And then you are surprised that they sabotage them.

Carla: Yes, I understand.

Dr. Prata: And so, for the moment, we can't do family therapy because you aren't ready for it.

Aldo: (*Kindly*) We don't know your terms or your postulate. Therapy presupposes that there are no anomalous roles in the family. So you tell us that we can't have therapy because Carla's role is not the traditional one, but that she plays an anomalous, atypical role . . .

Dr. Prata: If she only had an atypical role! True, Carla has been placed in the role of *paterfamilias* but we also feel that she has a deep emotional attachment to that role.

Marco: Dr. Prata, do you mean that even if we were to carry on with the therapy, nothing would happen? What does "ready" mean?

Dr. Prata: It means that family therapy is indicated because there is a great discomfort here, but we can't because Carla isn't ready.

Marco: And that holds you back.

Aldo: Carla would curb the efficiency of the therapy.

Marco: What I want to know is whether it would be too hard for Carla or whether it would hold up the therapy.

Dr. Prata: It's too hard on Carla.

Marco: So there you are!

Dr. Prata: Inasmuch as Carla is not yet ready to change her role.

Marco: I understand.

Dr. Prata: Because she gets such a gratification from it. She is used to being the one who, even though she may be suffering, decides and acts. That may upset her but it gratifies her. It makes her suffer but also lends her prestige. From the age of eight, and now she is 30, she has been playing an important role. She has become completely identified with that role; thus she is not ready to drop it. That's why we must leave it there.

Mrs. Mina: (*Skeptically*) Carla, does that convince you?

Anna: How will you be able to tell that Carla is ready? Because she might be ready in six years' time or she might never be!

Dr. Prata: Some things between you will have to change. That would take you at least six months, but perhaps things will never change. I can't tell.

Anna: What must Carla do to find herself?

Dr. Prata: She's no fool. She is a girl given to introspection. She will feel it inside when she is ready to drop her salvational role. Carla, your interventions have saved many situations, and so you don't want to renounce that role and the esteem you derive from it.

Carla: You are wrong to say I have played that role ever since the age of eight. I've only had it since I was 23.

Mrs. Mina: Before, because you were the firstborn!

Dr. Prata: You keep on changing your dates, Mrs. Mina. You said: "At the age of five she was a big girl already, and when she was eight I went out to work and left the children in her charge."

Carla: Yes, that's quite true. But the role I have now is worse than the one I had first. I remember precisely when I took it on and how.

Dr. Prata: When you were 23, you said.

Carla: Yes. When my mother's mother died. There was a whole gang of aunts who got nothing done and then there was me. As Aldo put it, there was the whole feminine clan.

Dr. Prata: Did you inherit your new role?

Carla: Yes, but it wasn't just that. That lot was very emotional and very ineffective. I felt the need, very strongly, to get myself accepted by these women as a very strong, intelligent, very successful person. We had been kept out of my mother's family because they disapproved of her marriage. When my grandmother died, I decided that I would become part of their clan. In the circumstances, I was very efficient, a fact the clan acknowledged and of which my aunts availed themselves. I have become so efficient that, in emergencies, even at work, I can handle any crisis, I don't panic, I act.

Dr. Prata: Of course. You are so used to it that you never lose your cool. There is nothing negative about that. In fact, it is most positive.

Carla: But I don't think anyone could forget that if someone has behaved exemplarily for 10 years, then the others don't spit in his face when he stops behaving in that way. (*Turns to her family*) Don't I get any reaction from you? If they were to take the weight off me, I wouldn't be losing any prestige!

Dr. Prata: Those are words. I prefer to base myself on this session.

Carla: On people's faces.

Dr. Prata: Certainly. On their expressions, their tears. And I take responsibility for my decisions. The team said: "In this family there is much discomfort and many problems resulting from her playing that . . . forgive me, 'false role.' "

Carla: I understand.

Dr. Prata: A role that doesn't belong to you as you can see in the Register of Births and Deaths. It fell to you through a chain of circumstances. The other members of the family have become used to not playing their proper roles because you have assumed responsibility for everything. And you have completely identified yourself with that salvational role. (*Carla and Mrs. Mina laugh.*)

Mrs. Mina: (*Sarcastically*) May I say something?

Dr. Prata: Now you all laugh as your family is used to!

Mrs. Mina: Luckily!

Dr. Prata: Yes, Mrs. Mina, but this is not a matter to make light of.

Mrs. Mina: We aren't making light of it.

Dr. Prata: Carla is sad. Aldo, Marco, and Anna are sad. Mama is furious. Ciro is disturbed and disturbing. And you continue to play your "chronic" roles. We have been discussing the indications in favor of family therapy. It's impossible to proceed with it because Carla is not ready.

Mrs. Mina:	On the practical level, if Carla were to abdicate and to shed the burden of the bambini (*sic!*) what would happen then? Because we have that problem, you see, and the problem is not Ciro; the problem is the family *and* Ciro.
Dr. Prata:	The day Carla is ready, there will be changes.
Mrs. Mina:	So you think that Carla ought to say: "I'll let go of everything"?
Anna:	No, because none of us can step into her shoes.
Mrs. Mina:	And what about Ciro?
Marco:	None of us children should deal with Ciro.
Carla:	Everyone will adjust.
Mrs. Mina:	That's what I want to know from you.
Dr. Prata:	I am not telling anybody to wash their hands of anything.
Mrs. Mina:	(*Ironically*) But what must Carla do to get a different attitude? How is the practical problem of Ciro going to be solved?
Dr. Prata:	That practical problem will be solved the moment Carla stops playing her present role. If she does, there will be changes. Don't ask me: "What should Carla do, what should we do?" When Carla changes her role, all the other roles will change as well and I should like you to let me know how things stand in six months' time. At the moment, Carla is saying: "Mine is a very hard role to play!" I believe her. But still it *also* gratifies her and so, for the time being, she clings to it.
Mrs. Mina:	So there is no solution.
Marco:	Mama, drop it!
Dr. Prata:	Mrs. Mina, you have understood me very well.
Mrs. Mina:	Forgive me, but I haven't.
Dr. Prata:	You have understood me perfectly. In any case, Marco will explain it. Good evening!

Follow-up—February 15, 1988

Each member of this family called several times after the second session (October 15, 1985), saying that I was wrong. They *needed* family therapy, I should not leave them in such trouble! At least I should do individual therapy with Carla and Ciro. I listened to them but remained firm in my decision. Marco was the one complaining most. Mrs. Mina was the one swearing most and was being aggressive in her request. Finally, she took Ciro to a psychoanalyst, whom she phoned before and after each session. Obviously, Ciro rejected him and the therapist gave up. Mrs. Mina insisted on having Ciro under heavy medication, which he would accept only once in a while. Ciro called me to get the address of a community, the farther away the better. The address I gave him was in Turin, but he joined a community in Sicily instead.

On February 15, 1988, Carla phones. She was more simpática than ever; her voice had lost all trace of sadness. Here is the information she gave me.

In November 1987, she decided that she was tired of carrying and pushing her husband and family. She joined a group of artists and, *alone*, went to Mexico to an international meeting. She was enthusiastic about this cultural experience, which connected her with interesting people from Latin America. When the meeting ended, she decided to stay. She was not yet ready to go home. She visited Mexico, the Yucátan, and Guatemala. Finally, she went home, determined to write. A magazine accepted the articles she wrote on Latin American artists and culture. She wanted to become a journalist and return to Latin America. Laughing, Carla said that, "under my instigation," she rented a small apartment in Milan, where she was planning to come, very often, with her husband. Their marriage had not improved much because "There is no hope for Aldo, he is still searching for a nanny."

Anna: She is very well and works a lot. She is 33 and lives with a 26-year-old lover. They are happy. She goes home very seldom, but has endless disputes with her mother.

Marco: Carla found him a small apartment to share with a friend in Milan. He has not gotten his diploma and works only every now and then. She constantly pushes him to study. He says "yes, yes" and does nothing. He is constantly "begging" for money to buy food and pay the rent. She already gave him more than three million but he has never given back a single penny. Now Carla has put an end to that. I suggested that she ask Marco to pay back the loan and she agreed.

Mrs. Mina and Ciro: She rented a newsstand under Ciro's name. On the appointed day for starting that business, Ciro said that he was too anxious to be able to work there. Mrs. Mina started making a "scenario": She was ill, she would die, and so on. At this point, Carla declared: "I'm not planning to open your newsstand. If you don't feel up to working there, rent it!" At this, Ciro replied angrily: "Rather than renting it, I prefer going there myself."

The same day, Carla left for Mexico. Two months later, when she came back, Ciro was working and seemed perfectly normal. At first, Carla thought that he was still under medication, but he was not. Before she left, he had been anxious and excited at times, but since November, he *had been very well*, managing his newsstand and doing everything properly. He wanted to get his driver's license and buy a car. He now has good relationships with his customers. During his spare time he plays basketball and tills a piece of land he's rented. When Mrs. Mina makes a "scenario" saying that she is about to die, Ciro is kind to her, gives her a glass of water, but doesn't get involved or become anxious and agitated as he used to.

Dr. Prata:	Is he still deaf?
Carla:	(*Laughing*) Oh yes, *he is deaf*! But his newsstand is at such a traffic intersection that nobody outside or inside the newsstand can hear a word. Ciro, who is used to reading people's lips, appears to be the only one hearing! (*She laughs*)
Dr. Prata:	Why did you phone me?
Carla:	Because I was happy with the news and knew you would be pleased with it.
Dr. Prata:	Right! (*We exchange cordial greetings.*)

Comment: It took a long time, but finally this family appeared to be out of the swamps and into a better life system.

Concluding Remarks

The script of families with a "Prestigious Sibling" can vary, but what continues to emerge from my research is that roles and "games" basically do not change. This is a real blessing because the "Prestigious Sibling Game" not only can be so perfectly camouflaged that it becomes difficult to uncover but can also originate authentic catastrophes when the camouflaging maneuver is successful.

If at the end of the second session, we still have doubts about whether they are playing the "Prestigious Sibling Game" or not, we invite the family to a third consultative session. Finally, if we cannot reach a firm conclusion, I would tell the family that many things have come to the open, but to make a decision, it's better to meet again within six months. I prefer to "wait and see" rather than to prescribe family therapy and ruin them. It's amazing to see that even when the social and cultural backgrounds of the families are diverse, the peculiarities of the "gamblers" remain remarkably similar. Let's see these peculiarities starting with the last generation.

The Designated Patient appears to be not only seriously disturbed but disturbing, too. Usually, he has been hospitalized, or in any case has received batteries of tests and different pharmacological and psychological treatments.

The "Prestigious Sibling" looks smart, elegant, well off, and "simpático."

The Other Siblings, if any, are usually insignificant, pathetic, sometimes symptomatic characters. They seem incapable, in their studies and work, of reaching the level of their "Prestigious Sibling" and are thus dissatisfied with their own lives.

The parents are in a conflict which could carefully be hidden.

The husband can "officially" be insane, as in the *Mina family*, where he played the madman so successfully that he very capably obtained a 100 percent disablement pension *and* an apartment from the municipality.

In other cases, the husband could behave normally at work and speak and act like a fool only at home and at the therapy sessions (Selvini Palazzoli, 1983; Haley, 1986). These men's peculiar similarities are that they are completely disqualified. Regarding their families of origin, they often are "orphans," having no relatives at all or having no contact whatsoever with them. Either they were already underestimated people or they received their disqualification mark once and forever from their in-laws and their own family the very day they got married.

When they are not "orphans," sometimes there is a crossing disqualification to the man for marrying *that* woman and to the woman for marrying *that* man.

Usually, the message which is constantly sent to the husband by the in-laws and by the wife means that he can do nothing to achieve an acceptable status. Sometimes, before getting married, he may have been successful in his studies or profession. Then, as if ground down under the weight of this merciless disapproval, he becomes the "loser" character we encounter in the therapy room.

The husband, full of acrimony and bitterness, couldn't or wouldn't do anything effective to change his role in the "game." On the contrary, the impression he gives is that of wanting to take his disqualification to an extreme, even to a grotesque extreme. Finally, he becomes "unreliable." Actually, that situation could be reversed and applied to the wife, but it's unusual.

The Wife: The husband's disqualification was so devastating that even the wife received the infectious inoculation simply by marrying such a bad choice.

Her usual way of facing a disqualification is "active" instead of "passive." She doesn't appear overcomed by the disqualification. She counteracts by becoming an energetic and, seemingly, domineering character.

If the husband dies, the wife is directly exposed to the family's disqualification. She, then, becomes the "bad choice." She might react by making the "depression" move. In that case, family therapy could be requested to treat her, and her depression could make it more difficult for the therapist to uncover the "Prestigious Sibling Game."

In the other cases, the husband continues playing the "unreliable" character, with the wife trying to play the "reliable" one, at least concerning practical matters.

She is disqualified as he is, but her situation seems less unbearable because, momentarily, she could hope against hope to share some prestige and power with the "crown heir." Against hope because that "crown" was placed on her son or daughter's head by a member of the *first generation,* usually a grandmother backed by the entire women's clan. Nothing changes even when this grandmother dies. The clan will continue to disqualify the parents, giving prestige to their son or daughter, pushing him/her to assume all the responsibilities in the family and to fulfill the clan's expectations.*

On the contrary, at this changing historical phase, men's gaming field is larger, seeing that it includes work, family, sport, politics, and so on. They also have more cultural and economic power. It could be interesting to investigate the "Prestigious Sibling Game" in a different culture.

At a certain point the hierarchical levels are so upset that the situation becomes unbearable. A sibling starts presenting unsuitable behavior and the clan responds by placing the entire fault on the parents' inadequacy. Husband and wife start accusing each other and consequently they become even more inefficient as a couple. The family rely heavily on the "crown heir," who receives a distressing load of responsibilities and will call for help, sooner or later. If we agree to engage in that family therapy, which the latter has requested, we side with him, with the clan, disqualifying the parents, implementing the "Prestigious Sibling's" authority (and burden), and subscribing to the notion that he/she is on a different level, higher than the siblings *and the parents.*

One should not be surprised at having to face the dissent of the family when one changes their entire politics. The fact is that one is upsetting the "game," turning upside down all the roles of the family members. It will take a while for the parents to understand that the "systemic jolt" was not given against them. When positive changes finally occur in the family, the parents will succeed, without any explanation, in recognizing that actually the therapist was acting properly since he was restoring the hierarchy and reinstating them, at long last, in their parental role.

---

*It seems to me that men usually do not form clans giving an heir the power. When a man of the first generation has power, he keeps it for himself. For women, the gaming field is often limited to the house and the family. For this reason, they tend to bank more on the family's relations.

7

Adoptive Parents: Their Particular Problem and Problems Created by the Specialists

In my opinion, when family therapy is advisable, the New Method is never dangerous. However, there are cases where this technique proves useless, as in "antisocial families," or not suitable, as in "adoptive families."

"Antisocial families" give the impression that they are living in a totally disturbed way with respect to moral rules, hierarchies, everyday life habits, schedules, money, and so on. Relationships with outsiders seem to be superficial and conflicting.

The relationship with the therapist is fragmentary because each member of the family devotes himself to pulling it apart. Such families may show, through their apparent enthusiasm and openly cheerful attitude, how happy they are to see the therapist. Or else, being just as noisy, they may show irritated and polemic reactions towards everything: the institution, the time set for the appointment, the appointment itself, the therapist, and more. In spite of a certain repetitiveness in the formal approach, it seems that there is never a real contiuum between one session and the following one. It probably does exist, but it is something that the therapist does not perceive and cannot work on.

Of course, those families are "natural groups with their own histories," but they don't give the impression of being such entities or, at least, of being the kind of group we normally mean, seeing that they seem to be living according to present impulses without having a past or a future. They remind me of those movies in which the various scenes which follow each other can only in an arbitrary way be defined as "film sequences" because they appear to be totally disconnected from each other. They actually ought to be called "shots," which would be more appropriate. Sometimes these "shots" look alike, but it seems that they have been filmed without a script, at different points in time, with different motivations and aims.

Trying to create links between the various stages of a session, as well as between sessions, is a difficult and almost hopeless task. If one member of the family shows dismay or suffering, as soon as the therapist tries to take advantage of this frame of mind and use it in order to find some anchorage point and then a way in to enter the family pattern, all of a sudden everything changes and the therapist receives a diametrically opposed message. In "antisocial families," despite the weariness—including physical weariness—which derives from constantly living in such a situation, it appears that the *unwillingness* to accept the rules set by an outsider is stronger than the *willingness* to collaborate with a view to a change (Watzlawick, Weakland, & Fish, 1974).

An "antisocial family" is always an insubordinate family (Viaro & Leonardi, 1982). The only rule the family members obey is that of not obeying any rule. Consequently, the therapist will never succeed in setting a therapeutic context. He will have to make and remake the therapeutic contract only to see it broken repeatedly. The family will not allow the therapist to conduct a session or treatment properly.

The New Method is definitely based on a contract, rules, and prescriptions, but "antisocial families" are delighted to break each and every one repeatedly. I think every therapist understands what I mean. They are so accustomed to disqualifying therapists and prescriptions that even breaking the *secret* will remain without consequences. After the three-and-a-half years of experience I had with them in Switzerland, I can report that they really are extremely discouraging people. I pity therapists who are obliged to confront such cases, but I have no practical suggestions for them. Anyway, with or without the New Method, I was unable to break any "antisocial game." Moreover, I am quite determined never to repeat this depressing experience.

Concerning "adoptive families," the New Method could be suitable, but the parents, regardless of the children's age, usually do not follow the "prescription." I have tried with the most motivated families, with parents at their wits' end, but always in vain. When I prescribe the *evening disappearances*, the parents reply that they could never obey this prescription and leave the children alone. They become grim, give evasive answers, and come back having done nothing. They don't say: "Look Doctor, they are our adopted children, we don't have the courage it takes. If they were our children we could do anything." They don't say so because, although *the children are theirs*, there is still something special about them. When I insist on the necessity of following the prescription, they refuse and drop out.

Even after many years, such parents probably feel a greater and different type of responsibility from that of natural parents. Even though they may trust the therapist, they don't feel up to following through a prescription that implies granting the children greater independence and responsibility. The fact is that they have guilt feelings at the very thought of any mishap or discomfort their children might suffer.

THE BERTIN FAMILY

This was one of the adoptive families I had to deal with. I report this case because the problem and other difficulties I had with them should never be underevaluated by a specialist. The family was composed of four members: the parents and two adopted children. The Bertins were in their 40s and had attended four years of grade school. Mr. Bertin was a lathe operator and she was a housewife. Mrs. Bertin phoned the center because Sandro, age 11, was a bed wetter and couldn't read or write. His little sister, Claudia, age seven, did well at school, but was extremely lazy at home. The Bertins hadn't been able to conceive any children of their own.

The referring person was a psychiatrist at the hospital Sandro had been going to for gym lessons for the past five years. This doctor didn't seem particularly involved in the family's problems, so we didn't consider it necessary to contact him directly.

The Bertins seemed highly motivated about family therapy and yet, despite all my efforts, I was unable to make any headway with this family. I asked them why they had adopted *two* children, and the answer was that during the first six years of their marriage they had always had some relatives or others staying with them. When these finally left, they started feeling terribly lonely and unhappy. Mr. Bertin would spend his evenings in bars and Mrs. Bertin was so miserable that she'd cry for days on end.

After a year spent living like that, they decided they'd adopt two children to relieve their loneliness and give their life meaning. Sandro, their first child, was eight months old when he was adopted. Claudia was two months old when she joined them, and Sandro was then three-and-a-half years old. He welcomed her warmly. Sandro was diagnosed with a cardiac problem when he was three years old and the cardiologist told his parents: "You must never contradict him or thwart him in any way. Don't make him cry or get angry."

The Bertins followed the doctor's orders and Sandro grew up as a terribly spoiled child. A few years later, another cardiologist reported the boy's heart to be perfectly healthy. He said that the cardiac problem was a figment of the other specialist's imagination. "Sandro's only problem is that he's too flabby—he needs exercise." The Bertins were very surprised, but they continued spoiling Sandro as they had before and, to be fair, they spoiled Claudia as well. However, all the while the parents were complaining about their children's intolerable behavior, they kept smiling warmly and encouragingly at them. Mr. Bertin said: "It's a difficult situation we're in, especially since Sandro still can't get dressed or do anything on his own."

The atmosphere was heavy during the session. There was this obvious but puzzling contradiction between everyone's verbal and nonverbal behavior. Apparently, no one had strong-armed this family into requesting therapy. It was true that the parents had a list of complaints about Sandro, but what, then, was amiss between them and me? Did they by any chance get the idea that Sandro was retarded due to some irreversible physical impairment? This is a question I always ask before I undertake family therapy, and in this particular case it seemed absolutely indispensable. So, I asked first Mr. Bertin, then his wife, whether, in their opinion, Sandro was mostly lazy or if he was physically and psychologically impaired. Mr. Bertin answered straight away: "Sandro's problem is 70 percent laziness and 30 percent real difficulties." Mrs. Bertin flashed a bright smile at her son and said: "Sandro is just 100 percent lazy, that is all!"

Were they requesting family therapy as a cure for laziness? I was still hopelessly in the dark. Mr. and Mrs. Bertin obviously doted on their children and accepted the fact that they were lazy, even though they complained about it. The only time Mrs. Bertin sounded exasperated was when she started telling me about the special remedial gym classes that she'd been taking Sandro to, twice a week, for five long years. I decided to have them come to a second session, to probe more deeply into the couple's lonely years prior to the adoption. My idea was to wrap up this second session by congratulating Sandro on his reluctance to grow up, due to his awareness of his parents' fear at the idea of being left alone and leading a meaningless life.

During the second session, it emerged that after their first year of loneliness and constant bickering, Sandro's arrival on the scene had been a veritable godsend to his mother: "All my sadness disappeared, as though by magic. Suddenly my husband was always at my side, helping me . . . we were so happy!" "However, lately, my wife has started getting overly anxious every time Sandro is two minutes behind schedule. Because, you see, Sandro and Claudia have started going out with their friends, now." Could they possibly have come to see me because their children were getting too independent? Sandro's teachers were complaining that he was never doing a thing at school. At home his mother was always at his beck and call. Mr. Bertin said that his wife had a "heart made of butter," whereas he would have liked to be somewhat more severe. "I can't interfere, even though I don't always agree with my wife."

At this point I had to make a decision. I left the children at home and invited only the parents to the third session.

Since the symptoms didn't look very serious and there appeared to be a difference of opinion about educational methods, I decided to give the parents the prescription we had called "Odd Days and Even Days" (Selvini Palazzoli et al., 1978b). I hadn't used this prescription for three years, since, in the meantime, I had worked out more effective ones. When I referred to the written text of this prescription, I became aware of a huge theoretical error in it. The therapist assigns to one of the siblings the task of observing and writing down, over a month, how his or her parents carry out the prescription. By enlisting a sibling as coworker, the therapist raises him or her above the level of the other children and even above that of the parents. Since respecting and restoring family hierarchy was always foremost in our minds, it amazed me to think that we could have disregarded such a basic principle (Selvini Palazzoli et al., 1977; Selvini Palazzoli, 1981). However, we had!

So, the prescription I gave the Bertins was a modified version of the one we had previously published, and it read: "On even weekdays, that is Tuesday, Thursday, and Saturday, starting tomorrow and up to our next session, between the hours of . . . and . . . (a time we made sure that the whole family would be home), anything Sandro or Claudia do—whether they fail to wash themselves, get dressed, do their homework, prepare their satchels for school, etc.—Dad will decide what has to be done about it. Mom has to keep out of things entirely and act as though she wasn't there." On odd days—Monday, Wednesday, Friday—during that same time interval, Mom will be the sole judge of what has to be done about everything concerning Sandro and Claudia, and Dad has to behave "as if he wasn't there." Each parent, on their assigned day, has to note down on a dated sheet of paper any failure of the "off-duty" parent to comply with the "I'm-not-really-here" rule. I assigned this prescription, and again invited only the parents to the fourth session.

Mr. and Mrs. Bertin showed up for the fourth session very upset and dissatisfied. Mr. Bertin promptly demanded a certificate stating exactly how long therapy would last, claiming he intended to get a refund from Social Security for the expenses. Mrs. Bertin reported that everything had been going haywire since they'd started therapy. Then they got down to complaining about me, although they hadn't done a single thing to cooperate.

At this stage I thought I might be dealing with the typical welfare family which, having adopted two children, considers themselves entitled to every possible help free of charge. Therefore, I decided to use the certificate they were requesting to increase their responsibility. I told them the certificate would also include how effectively they were following my precription. At this, Mr. Bertin shot right back: "All right, Doctor, but what happens if we carry out your prescription and nothing changes?" Taken by surprise I blurted out: "To begin with, start by carrying out the prescription."

I dictated the "Odd Days and Even Days" prescription again, since they couldn't remember what they'd done with the text I'd given them the last time. Mrs. Bertin began writing down my instructions eagerly, whereas Mr. Bertin started hedging and trying to angle a reduction of his "Even Days" obligations, hoping to get away with only an hour and a half per day, that is, from dinnertime (7 P.M.) to when the kids went off to bed (8:30).

The Notes they produced at the fifth session were absolutely disqualifying. They were illegible and, furthermore, didn't make sense. However, one thing was clear: Mr. and Mrs. Bertin had failed to understand what behavior they had been expected to check on. They could see nothing really objectionable in anything their children did or didn't do. So, it finally struck me that this family had *only* come because Sandro's teachers had complained about his behavior to the school psychologist, who then referred him to the consulting psychiatrist. This specialist, then, had simply foisted the family off on me. Sandro's school record was his teacher's problem, nobody else's. The bed wetting certainly wasn't a serious issue, since his parents only had to wake him up and make him urinate before they went to bed.

At this point I told the Bertins we had at long last realized what a huge catastrophe this therapy had been for their family and that we had decided to put an end to all this torture. Their mood changed instantly: Both parents smiled, relaxed, and nodded in agreement. I was right, they said. They were perfectly satisfied with their lives. Their children were used to having Mrs. Bertin make all the decisions, so when Mr. Bertin—as per our prescription—started taking over Mrs. Bertin's role and Mrs. Bertin began pretending she was a statue of salt, the kids got bewildered and very angry. Mr. Bertin enjoyed being waited on hand and foot by his wife, and she, in turn, enjoyed waiting on all of them. "Doctor, I even gave up my job at the factory in order to look after them properly! Please don't worry about Sandro—he is such a sociable child; he has lots of friends. He only refuses to read and write—so what? He balks at doing these things for himself, but he's perfectly willing to help Claudia with her homework. He has his heart set on becoming a chef, and he's had too much schooling as it is." Now that I'd finally stopped persecuting them, Mr. and Mrs. Bertin actually became very affectionate, very reassuring, and volunteered all the information I could possibly want.

As in so many instances, this family's problem had been brought on by specialists. First, the cardiologist with his improper diagnosis and instructions had impaired the parents' self-confidence and spontaneity. This ushered in a breakdown in Sandro's relationship with his parents. Like all adoptive parents, the Bertins were terrified of doing something wrong, so they never questioned the first specialist's orders and scrupulously followed them for years: "To be really good parents, you must avoid crossing Sandro in any way and have his condition checked periodically, without fail." The second cardiologist then prescribed gym lessons, and the school psychiatrist family therapy. Each specialist, including myself, had done his bit to throw a wrench into the works.

We specialists never stop to consider the torture we inflict on mothers and offspring when we prescribe a reeducational scheme that requires them to stop their normal lives twice or three times a week, over a number of years, to carry out our request. Even the most loving of mothers can't help getting furious at a therapist and, overtly or covertly, taking it out on her child. The child can't fail to eventually loathe a mother who drags him away from his friends to a long, tiresome reeducation session which he hates. The least he can do in revenge is to wet his bed!

We therapists must be more careful with all our diagnosing and prescribing because we are the most dangerous originators of psychological and psychosomatic disorders. We are incredibly cavalier about arousing anxiety and introducing distortions into parents' and children's relationships.

In the case of the Bertins, the therapy ended on a note of mutual trust and understanding. I phoned them three years later (Prata, 1988) to ask how the family was getting on. Mrs. Bertin told me that right after our last meeting she had courageously quit both the hospital checkups and gym classes. Six months later she went to the hospital for a hysterectomy and while she was away the children grew more self-reliant. Since then, they have been cooperative and eager to help around the house. A week after our last session, Sandro had stopped wetting his bed. He was doing well at school and trying his best to complete school as quickly as possible to start training as a chef. Claudia was well, and life in the family was peaceful and pleasant.

8

Concluding Remarks

After working for six years in Switzerland and doing a five-month training course in England, as well as a seven-month training course in the U.S.A., I returned to Milan, where Mara Selvini Palazzoli invited me to join her team. I worked with her for 14 years, until June 1985, doing clinical work, research, and writing, mainly on anorexia nervosa and psychosis. Then, it came to a point where I couldn't go on any longer in that setting.

Colleagues who admire Mara asked me how I survived the separation and overcame the loss. I was certainly depressed, but to my great surprise the most difficult thing was to exit from the "mental system" we had formed together after Boscolo and Cecchin had left. I felt, somehow, like a half brain disconnected from its other part (Ashby, 1954; Morin, 1973). Therefore, I did something drastic in reaction. I went to Ireland with Biba, my 14-year-old niece, and hitchhiked from Galway to Donegal, then to Malin Head.

I had had the impression that Ireland was beautiful, with fewer tourists than other countries and a light rain possibly three times a day. Well, the summer of 1985 was the most rain drenched this country had ever had. In fact, the government had to decree subsidies due to the loss of the harvest and livestock. Obviously, the tourists fled, but we bravely held out. The landscape was marvelous and the kindhearted Irish felt sorry we had such a bad weather. No tourists meant there were few cars around for hitchhikers. Moreover, there were very few buses since the Irish were on holiday as well. And with the deluge, as soon as one left a major highway, one walked or one drowned. I discovered that the little picturesque ponds on the map took an entire day to go around, carrying a backpack with only blackberries and raspberries to eat. The cows and donkeys who were standing in the water looked me in the eye with mutual understanding. To get somewhere in the evening, soaked through, and find a "bed and breakfast" and a hot soup was the main problem.

I remember perfectly the day of my recovery. In the morning, to escape the rain, we took shelter under the roof of a newsstand. The headlines were about AIDS, and the news vendor was shouting that the Pope was right, this was God's curse "for their sins." Like Gavroche, in *Les Miserables* by Victor Hugo, I preferred to reenter dans la Rue. In the afternoon, after only one lift and 13 kilometers on foot, a car passed us by without stopping but showered me with a bath of mud from head to foot. I had a "bellissima" hysterical crisis and started screaming at the cars which were not stopping and at myself for not staying in sunny Italy. Instead, I had journeyed to Ireland to be soaked with all that rain during *my holidays*! Then I turned around and saw Biba clutching a stone fence and rolling with laughter. First I hated her and then I started laughing heartily; I was cured.

I warmly recommend Ireland to those people who, due to relational, contextual, hierarchical, and other problems, have to leave the field (Morin 1977; Selvini Palazzoli, 1985a; Selvini Palazzoli et al., 1987). Ireland sees and provides.

When I returned to Milan with my brain washed and cleared, I opened my center, and in September 1985 started to work with Luisa Bigoni Prata. She had trained for three years with Drs. Boscolo and Cecchin (1977–1980), had done three years of workshop with me, and had been for a year the camerawoman at the Nuovo Centro. She had been working for many years with families, both in private practice and for public institutions in Bologna, where she lives.

Within a few weeks, Dr. Maria Vignato joined us. She had completed five years of training in macrosystems at the Nuovo Centro with Drs. L. D'Ettorre and I. Pisano and two years of workshop with me. She had previously worked for many years in public services and she is the director of a private center in Verona.

As I have said earlier, "The disadvantage of being a researcher working in a private center is to have a small number of cases. The advantage is the possibility to give each family all the time it needs without having to run from one family to another. Then, having the time to discuss that family at length and review the tape of the session creates a 'memory' which helps one, even after many years, to recognize and make connections with other cases presenting similarities. It facilitates, in an operative way, the streamlining of the investigative procedure, making more precocious and precise interventions on the family 'game' " (Prata, 1989, p. 125).

To overcome this handicap of too few cases to effectively control new hypotheses and new interventions, I decided to have regular workshops. To the French workshop I had been doing since 1979, I added one in Italian in September 1985.

Both groups gather 16 participants, who come to the center for six weekends per year. Since what I do are workshops and not training sessions, they have an unlimited duration. I have been working together with some colleagues for seven years. The fundamental prerequisite for admission is to be actively working with patients and, if possible, with families.

I have a telephone interview for admission and then select the participants. After working with them for a year, I make a second selection. Certain people, in spite of their intelligence and education, seem incapable of entering into a systemic way of thinking. I suggest that these individuals discontinue workshop attendance and, if possible, devote themselves to individual therapy.

The workshop program is the following: Saturday morning is dedicated to reading and discussing the transcript of a family session done at the center. In this way, each participant returns home with a session and with the notes taken during the discussion. On Saturday afternoon, we view on T.V. the most important sequences of that session. After this, the workshop members formulate their hypotheses on that "family game" and prepare the program for the following session with that family. If, in my opinion, it is a particularly instructive one, I present it in the next meeting. This may be a session which actually occurred a few years earlier, and it is interesting to compare their hypotheses and their planned program with ours as it actually took place. Nothing is said to the group regarding the following session or the progress and results of the therapy. In this way, one creates better participation and greater suspense.

At the beginning of the year I present cases which failed because they are more instructive and informative than those which go like oil on troubled waters, with a therapist in a state of grace, and a family which collaborates faithfully, putting into practice all the prescriptions. It seems to me fairer to show some therapeutic failures to colleagues who do their best but who—having less experience and working in less favorable conditions—collect more failures and more frustrations than we do. Besides, a wheel in which the cog does not function is much more stimulating and instructive than one which doesn't create any problem. After that, I show them sessions and therapies which went well. However, when I see their enthusiasm being replaced by discouragement, when they start saying that they would never be able to run the sessions as I do, I show them a total disaster, which makes everyone feel better.

Sunday morning is programmed to supervise three or four cases. The workshop members who present a case must distribute a photocopy of the telephone chart and also a summary of the previous sessions. In this way, the supervision is better structured. Obviously, each workshop is taped.

For the past seven years, I have worked with the Spanish group of Drs. Carmen Rojero and Teresa Suarez, with whom I meet yearly in Madrid. I'm particularly fortunate because the three groups, French, Spanish, and Italian, are very motivated and dynamically active. Since 80 percent of the participants work in the public sector, their help allows me to test hypotheses and interventions which I could never sufficiently test and check in my center alone. Without that help, my hypotheses and interventions could never have scientific value and could never be presented to clinicians and researchers.

Such testing has been done, for example, on the "Referring Sibling" (Selvini Palazzoli, 1985a), the "Germ Barrier" (Prata, 1989), "The Withdrawal of the Significant Ones" (Prata, 1988), and the "Adoptive Parents" (Selvini Palazzoli & Prata, 1980). The results of the testing make me consider these hypotheses valid and suggest certain interventions for individual and family therapies.

References

Ashby, W. (1954). *Design for a Brain*. London: Chapman and Hall.

Ashby, W. (1958). *An Introduction to Cybernetics*. New York: John Wiley.

Bateson, G., Jackson, D.D., Haley, J., & Weakland, J.H. (1956). Toward a theory of schizophrenia. *Behavioral Science, 1*, 251–264.

Bateson, G. (1972a). *Steps to an Ecology of Mind*. San Francisco: Chandler.

Bateson, G. (1972b). The logical categories of learning and communication. In *Steps to an Ecology of Mind*. San Francisco: Chandler.

Bateson, G. (1972c). Form, substance and difference. In *Steps to an Ecology of Mind*. San Francisco: Chandler.

Bateson, G. (1979). *Mind and Nature: A Necessary Unity*. New York: E.P. Dutton.

Berne, G. (1964). *Games People Play*. New York: Grove Press.

Bertalanffy (von) L. (1968). *General System Theory*. New York: George Braziller.

Crozier, M., & Friedberg, E. (1977). *L'Acteur et le Système*. Paris: Editions du Seuil.

Di Blasio, P., Fischer, J.M., & Prata, G. (1986). The telephone chart: A cornerstone of the first interview with the family. *Journal of Strategic and Systemic Therapies*, Special Issue on Interviewing, *V* (1–2), 31–44.

Foerster (von) H. (1981). *Observing Systems*. Seaside, CA: Intersystems Publications.

Haley, J. (1959). The family of the schizophrenic: A model system. *Journal of Nervous and Mental Disease, 129*, 357–374.

Haley, J. (1963). *Strategies of Psychotherapy.* New York: Grune & Stratton.

Haley, J. (1967). Toward a theory of pathological systems. In G.H. Zuk and I. Boszormenyi-Nagy (Eds.), *Family Therapy and Disturbed Families.* Palo Alto: Science and Behavior Books.

Haley, J. (1971). *Changing Families: A Family Therapy Reader.* New York: Grune & Stratton.

Haley, J. (1976). *Problem-Solving Therapy.* San Francisco: Jossey-Bass.

Haley, J. (1986). *The Power Tactics of Jesus Christ and Other Essays.* New York: Triangle Press, distributed by Norton.

Hoffman, L. (1981). *Foundations of Family Therapy.* New York: Basic Books.

Jackson, D.D. (Ed.) (1960). *Etiology of Schizophrenia.* New York: Basic Books.

Jackson, D.D., & Haley, J. (1963). Transference revisited. *Journal of Nervous and Mental Diseases, 137,* 363–371.

Jackson, D.D. (1965). The study of family. *Family Process, 4* (1), 1–20.

Kaye, K. (1977). Toward the origin of dialogue. In H.R. Shaffer (Ed.), *Studies in Mother-Infant Interaction.* New York: Academic Press.

Keeney, B. (1983). *Aesthetics of Change.* New York: Guilford Press.

Khun, T.S. (1962). *The Structure of Scientific Revolution.* Chicago: The University of Chicago.

Lakatos, I. (1976). *Proofs and Refutations: The Logic of Mathematical Discovery.* Cambridge: Cambridge University Press.

Le Moigne, J.L. (1977). *La Théorie du Système Général. Théorie de la Modelisation.* Presses Univ. de France.

Mildefort, C.F. (1982). Use of the family in the treatment of schizophrenic and psychopatic patients. *Journal of Marital and Family Therapy, 8* (2), 1–11.

Minuchin, S. (1974). *Families and Family Therapy.* Cambridge: Harvard University Press.

Morin, E. (1973). *Le Paradigme Perdu: La Nature Humaine.* Paris: Editions du Seuil.

Morin, E. (1977). *La Méthode I. La Nature de la Nature.* Paris: Editions du Seuil.

Morin, E. (1980). *La Méthode II. La vie de la Vie.* Paris: Editions du Seuil.

Morin, E. (1982). *Science avec Conscience*. Paris: Fayard.

Morin, E. (1986). *La Méthode III. La connaissance de la Connaissance*. Paris: Editions du Seuil.

Neumann (von) J.V., & Morgenstern, O. (1944). *Theory of Games and Economic Behavior*. New York: Princeton University Press.

Popper, K.R. (1963). *Conjectures and Refutations*. New York: Harper.

Prata, G. (1983a). Un cas de dépression conjugale avec idée de suicide de la femme. *Thérapie Familiale, 4* (1). Génève.

Prata, G. (1983b). Conflit conjugal avec tentative de suicide du mari. *Thérapie Familiale, 4* (2). Génève.

Prata, G. (1987). The absent member maneuver at the first session of consultation. How to avoid making irreparable mistakes. *Journal of Strategic and Systemic Therapies, 6* (3), 24–41.

Prata, G. (1988). *A Systemic Jolt to "Family Games." The "New Method."* Helsinki: Valtion Painatuskeskus.

Prata, G. (1989). La Barriera di Microbi. In *Psicologia Clinica, Trattamenti in Setting di Gruppo* (pp. 125–136). Milano: Franco Angeli.

Raffin, C. (1988). Testing clinical hypotheses by means of "falsificationist epistemology." *Family Process, 27*, 485–489.

Russell, B. (1938). *Power: A New Social Analysis*. London: Unwin Books.

Searles, H. (1959). The effort to drive the other person crazy: An element in the etiology and psychotherapy of schizophrenia. *British Journal of Medical Psychology, 32*, 1–18.

Selvini Palazzoli, M. (1980). Why a long interval between sessions? The family-therapist suprasystem. In Andolfi, M., & Zwerling, I., (Eds.) *Dimensions of Family Therapy*. New York: The Guilford Press.

Selvini Palazzoli, M. (1981). *Self-Starvation*. New York: Jason Aronson.

Selvini Palazzoli, M. (1983). Jeu instigateur et symptôme psychotique. *Terapia Familiar y Comunitaria*. Lisboa: Proceedings of the International Congress.

Selvini Palazzoli, M. (1984). Behind the scenes of the organization: Some guidelines for the expert in human relations. *Journal of Family Therapy, 6*, 299–307.

Selvini Palazzoli, M. (1985a). The problem of the sibling as the referring person. *Journal of Marital and Family Therapy, 11*(1), 21–34.

Selvini Palazzoli, M. (1985b). "Que es la terapia del contexto?" Abordaje sistémico a los trastornos de conducta de la infancia y de la adolescencia. *Revista de la Asociacion Espanola de Neuropsiquiatria, 12.*

Selvini Palazzoli, M. (1986). Towards a general model of psychotic family games. *Journal of Marital and Family Therapy, 12* (4), 339–349.

Selvini Palazzoli, M., Anolli, L., Di Blasio, P, et al. (1987). *The Hidden Games of Organizations.* New York: Pantheon Books.

Selvini Palazzoli, M., Boscolo, L., Cecchin, G., & Prata, G. (1977). Family rituals. A powerful tool in family therapy. *Family Process, 16* (4).

Selvini Palazzoli, M., Boscolo, L., Cecchin, G., & Prata, G. (1978a). *Paradox and Counterparadox.* New York: Aronson.

Selvini Palazzoli, M., Boscolo, L., Cecchin, G., & Prata, G. (1978b). A ritualized prescription in family therapy. Odd days and even days. *Journal of Marriage and Family Counseling, 3–9.*

Selvini Palazzoli, M., Boscolo, L., Cecchin, G., & Prata, G. (1980a). The problem of the referring person. *Journal of Marital and Family Therapy, 6* (1), 3–9.

Selvini Palazzoli, M., Boscolo, L., Cecchin, G., & Prata, G. (1980b). Hypothesizing—Circularity—Neutrality: Three guidelines for the conductor of the session. *Family Process, 19* (1), 3–12.

Selvini Palazzoli, M., Carillo, M.S., & D'ettorre, L., et al., (1976). *Il Mago Smagato.* Milano: Feltrinelli.

Selvini Palazzoli, M., & Prata, G. (1980). Die macht der Onmacht. In J. Duss (von) Werdt, Welter Enderlin, R. (Eds.), *der Familienmensch.* Stuttgart: Klett-Cotta.

Selvini Palazzoli, M., & Prata, G. (1982a). A new method for therapy and research in the treatment of schizophrenic families. In Stierlin, H. Wynne, L.C., & Wirsching, M. (Eds.), *Psychosocial Intervention in Schizophrenia. An International View* (pp. 237–243). Berlin: Springer.

Selvini Palazzoli, M., & Prata, G. (1982b). Snares in family therapy. *Journal of Marital and Family, 8* (4), 443–450.

Selvini Palazzoli, M., & Viaro, M. (1988). The anorectic process in the family: A six-stage model as a guide for individual therapy. *Family Process, 27* (2), 129–148.

Selvini Palazzoli, M., et al. (1989). *Family Games.* New York: Norton.

Sluzki, C., & Veron, E. (1971). The double bind as a universal pathogenic situation. *Family Process, 10*, 397–417.

Speed, B. (1985). Evaluating the Milan approach. In Campbell, D., & Drape, R. (Eds.), *Applications of Systemic Family Therapy*. New York: Grune & Stratton.

Stanton, D. (1981). Strategic approaches to family therapy. In Gurman, A.S., & Kuykern, D.P. (Eds.), *Handbook of Family Therapy*. New York: Brunner/Mazel.

Viaro, M., & Leonardi, P. (1982). Le insubordinazioni, *Terapia Familiare, 12*, 41–63.

Viaro, M., & Leonardi, P. (1986). The evolution of an interview technique: A comparison between former and present strategy, *Journal of Strategic and Systemic Therapies, 5*, 14–30.

Watzlawick, P., Beavin, J.H., & Jackson, D.D. (1967). *Pragmatics of Human Communication*. New York: Norton.

Watzlawick, P., Weakland, J., & Fish, R. (1974). *Change: Principles of Problem Formation and Problem Resolution*. New York: Norton.

Wynne, L.C., & Thaler Singer, A. (1963). Thoughts disorders and the family relations of schizophrenics. *Archives of General Psychiatry, 9*, 191–206 and *12*, 187–220.

Index

is not psychoanalysis, 6, 9–11
is not suitable, 11
needed but . . . , 65
on the secret, 88–92
on the testing of motivations, 85–86
prescription for the Casta family, 45
prescription for the G.B. family, 41–42
standard procedure, 3–6
the U.S., 15–16
therapist's refusal, 139, 140, 142
when advisable, 155
Fear
    of germs, 36, 42
    of microbes, 34
    of thieves, 41
    Mrs. Casta's, 42, 43–44
Feedback
    instant, 59
    notes, 2, 95
    verbal and non-verbal, 88
Fiancé
    Bar family, 50
    family's favorable attitude, 138
    in conflict with future in-laws,
    Matta family, 26
    Sele family, 30, 73, 132–133
    the birthright, 137
First session, 5
    Proti family, 114–115
    usual procedure, 67–70
    with the Bar family, 48–59
    with the Bertin family, 157–159
    with the Casta family, 44
    with the G.B. family, 39–41
Fischer, J.M., 3; see also References
Freezing of the game, 9
Friends
    boyfriend and girlfriend, 72
    Sele family, 137
Frondizi Bullrich, S., 16

Game
    anorexic, 4
    antisocial, 159, 262
    autistic, 4
    dirty, xii
    family, 9–11, 14–15
    instigative, 24
    involved in, x
    mortiferous, 64
    ongoing, 4–6
    pathogenic, 9, 15
    prestigious sibling, 142
    psychotic, 4, 18
    relational, 136

G.B. family, 36–42
    first session, 39–41
General System Theory, 1
Germ barrier, 34–36, 38, 43–44
    testing of hypothesis, 167
Green table, x–xi, 14
    and the germ barrier, 35
    or gambling table, 20

Haley, J., 1; see also References
Hierarchy
    a basic principle, 160
    altered in hunger strike, 54
    confusion in the, 45, 49
    in a prestigious sibling game, 134
    Proti family, 121
Homeostasis, 15
    as a result, 45
    during the first session, 11
    family, 86
Hunger strike
    Bar family, 48, 50
    Bobby Sands, 50
    to alter the hierarchy, 55
Husband and wife
    in a prestigious sibling pattern, 152–154
    inadequacy, 34
    relationship, 46, 48, 50
    see also Couples
Hypothesis
    and the withdrawal of significant ones, 46,
        48, 59
    checking the, 11, 14
    gaming, 4
    initial, 17, 19
    main working, x
    testing of, 167
    with the Sele family, 70
"Hypothesizing—Circularity—Neutrality:
        Three Guidelines for the Conductor of the
        Session" (Selvini Palazzoli, et al.), 2
    first session, 69
Hysterectomy, 113, 163

Identified Patient, 4, 5, 7, 8, 15, 112;
    and the anorexic ploy, 12–13, 13
    and the disappearances, 92
    and the secret, 89–90, 91
    during first session, 68–69
    G.B. family, 37, 38
    paranoid, 18
Individual
    analysis, 30
    patients, ix
    therapy, 23, 48